Heartfelt Gratitude from Me to You

For as long as I can remember I have always loved to write. Ever since I was about eight years old and my parents bought me my first 'old school' vintage typewriter, I have been typing and writing away, starting many books with the dream of one day completing and publishing one. This first book is therefore, in addition to a labor of love and passion, truly a dream come true.

I would like to express my heartfelt gratitude to all the people in the universe, whom I love and adore for always supporting me in my many, many, many adventures which I have been so blessed and fortunate to have experienced, and continue to experience. I would like also thank YOU, the reader. By reading this, you play one of the main roles in this exciting adventure and realization of my dream.

If I achieve nothing more than to put a smile on your face, my goal is realized.

Last but not least I would like thank my parents, my sister, my husband, my extended family and friends, and most importantly the people who I draw the most inspiration from every day- the loves of my life- my three girls Leilani, Keona, and Mahniya. I say this all the time and I will say it now:

My darlings, although I gave birth to you, it is you who have truly given life and light to me, and you inspire me everyday to be the best version of myself. I love you with all my heart, soul, and being.

1

Table of Contents

Dedicated to the loves of my life
Leilani, Keona, & Mahniya

Editor: Laura Dal Farra
Cover design: Alexander von Ness

Preface

"You can't stop the waves but you can learn to surf." Jon Kabat-Zinn [i]

I started writing this book in one direction, but it eventually took on a life of its own, bursting open the Pandora's Box of my subconscious mind.

Not unlike most people, I have been through a plethora of experiences, some magical and euphoric, some dreadful and devastating. The latter was, for the most part, beyond my control. I did not choose the war. I did not choose the bombs that went off randomly throughout the day when I was seven years old. I did not choose to be bullied about my weight as a teen. I did not choose to be pointed at and to be called "foreigner" in middle school. I did not choose to be ridiculed in a foreign language in my 'foreign' high school. I did not choose the bomb scares while I was at university, which would lead to military car raids in the middle of the day. I did not choose to have fighter jets fly over my house (that were fired at from the ground), as I studied for my university final exams. I did not choose for my parents to separate, or to have them live on opposite sides of the globe. I did not choose to have a miscarriage. Nevertheless, I am alive, my parents are alive, I have three beautiful, healthy children; and at the end of the day, these are the essentials of my life: health and safety of those that I love. My heart overflows with happiness and gratitude.

As with most people however, there have been points in my life where I have felt pity for myself. Whenever this has occurred, I have brought myself back to a profound realization (but in reality, not so profound). Are you ready for your mind to be blown? You may need to sit down for this…

Almost every other human being in the universe has faced, is facing, or will face challenges.

It is how we respond to and deal with these challenges, which makes all the difference.

No one is immune to- or exempt from- hardships, struggles, or challenges. Social status, political status, economic status, academics, appearance – none of these makes you immune because alas, cancer does not discriminate, natural disasters do not discriminate, a sick parent who you are the caregiver for, did not ask to be sick. These are all a part of life, but they do not mean that we cannot – in spite of these - experience happiness.

I can honestly say my life is amazing. With a shift in perspective, it is clear to me that my experiences, good and bad, molded me into the person I am today; and I am grateful for all of them. I have traveled the world, lived in three continents and met hundreds if not thousands of people. I have an amazingly fulfilling career which I am so passionate about. Most significantly, I have a loving family and amazing friends, with the stars of the show being my three amazing children. Today, I strive, as most people do, to live a life of meaning, happiness, and love.

As I draw near the magical four-o, my eyes are open now-wider than ever- to the abundance of suffering in our world. But it's not all bad news.

I do not believe humankind is destined to desolate misery. I believe that happiness is attainable. While I may be an idealist, I do believe in the simplistic notion that happiness, love, and goodness are contagious. If this book accomplishes nothing more than making you even a little bit happier, I would have realized my goal.

Now that we have established that virtually anyone can be happy, I have more good news: happiness is an endless and FREE commodity, a well that never dries up. We can swim in it, bathe in it, and soak in it all day and all night! There will be times where it will rain buckets of happiness, but most times, it is up to us to keep dipping that bucket into the well to keep hydrated.

Who Wants to Be Happy?

I do not think anyone chooses to be unhappy. Why would they? In fact, it is my belief that after humans have acquired their basic needs, that is, food and shelter, otherwise known as the first level in Maslow's hierarchy of needs, most spend the rest of their lives in the pursuit of happiness. Unfortunately, it can feel like getting into a car and driving to cross the ocean: simply unattainable and impossible.

This begs the question:

What Exactly Is Happiness?

By definition, happiness is a mental or emotional state of well-being, characterized by pleasant emotions ranging from contentment to intense joy. A variety of biological, psychological, religious, and philosophical approaches have strived to define happiness and identify its sources. Various research groups, including positive psychology, endeavor to apply the scientific method to answer questions about what happiness is, and how it might be attained. Philosophers and religious thinkers often define happiness in terms of living a good life, or flourishing, rather than simply as an emotion. [ii]

What does that all really mean? What exactly does 'living a good life' entail?

I am of the humble opinion and belief that happiness cannot be defined as a single entity, nor should it be perceived as a destination. It is an infinite number of entities, which can develop into a lasting state of being happy. Therefore happiness is a bunch of little 'happies' (no, that is not a word) which can connect and lead to a lasting state of happiness. It is each of these 'happies' or entities, which I have coined as a Bliss Buzz.

1. Find Your Bliss Buzz

"You can shake the sand from your shoes but it will never leave your soul." Unknown

Find your bliss. I have come across this phrase repeatedly over the years and it has made me wonder:

Is bliss something that you can actually find?

Is it a destination?

Is it a single entity?

Could there be more than one type of bliss for each of us?

Bliss

Each person has his or her personal definition of bliss. For me, it's, for example, that moment my naked feet touch a sandy beach, the rush of the warm sand which begins at the soles of my feet then sweeps up with an ethereal force through my entire body. You know what I'm talking about: the feeling that is so delicious that it takes over your entire being. That is one of my Bliss Buzzes.

Buzz

What about the 'buzz'? In this book the term 'buzz' is used as a metaphor, however if I were to use an analogy to describe it, the most fitting would be wine. If you don't drink wine then insert coffee, tea, chocolate, a morning run, etc., all the things in your life that affect those special parts of the brain that seemingly alter your consciousness. For the wine enthusiasts (including yours truly), it would be like that first sip of chilled wine on a warm summer's day and the sensation of the wine as it smoothly caresses your tongue, glides down your throat, tickles your senses and warms your insides, leaving you with an ever so subtle 'ahhh moment'. That is my analogy of a buzz.

However, you do not need to drink wine to get it. The buzz is essentially a lingering state of metaphorical intoxication by a blissful moment or collection of moments, hence: The Bliss Buzz.

Bliss Buzz

In summary:

A Bliss Buzz is a positive experience that creates a blissful sensation with a lingering effect, stimulating the senses of the mind, body, and spirit.

As with an actual buzz, a Bliss Buzz will eventually wear off. But we have infinite opportunities to keep the buzz itself going simply by experiencing more Bliss Buzzes.

How Can We Get Bliss Buzzed?

A Bliss Buzz is the kind of thing either that can fall into your lap, or that you can seek out. Either way, it is a party we are all invited to. Anyone can get Bliss Buzzed!

For me, the list of Bliss Buzz opportunities is infinite. I find that the more I am aware of them, the more I tend to seek them out. There are some types of Bliss Buzzes, like being on a beach, which are common to most people. Then there are other types of Bliss Buzzes, like performing on stage in front of a large crowd, which I consider awesome, but to someone with extreme stage fright, it may sound more like a nightmare.

What is YOUR Bliss Buzz?

I'll show you mine if you show me yours.

I would like to share with you some of my favorite Bliss Buzzes, coupled with some fascinating physiological and psychological explanations of why they make me feel the way they do.

I would love it if you shared some of your Bliss Buzzes by journaling at the end of this book in the 'your turn' section. I hope that as you read on, you will be inspired to get your Bliss Buzz 'on' right now!

2. The Hippy Movement

"Kick off your shoes and feel the rhythm of your souls." Ioana Aboumitri

"When you dance, your purpose is not to get to a certain place on the floor. It's to enjoy each step along the way." Wayne Dyer [iii]

"Nobody cares if you can't dance well. Just get up and dance. Great dancers are not great because of their technique, they are great because of their passion." Martha Graham[iv]

I love to dance, I always have. Even though I have always had two left feet, I would still, as a teenager, close the door to my room and blast my "hippie music" (as my dad would call it) and dance for the love of it. You know what I'm talking about, that "dance like no one is watching" kind of dance; the 'no inhibitions' dance; the 'in the moment' awesome dance.

13

In 2007, I came out of hiding, as it were, and created Kelani Dance: a *Polynesian inspired; hip shakin'; body lovin'; chakra rockin'; program for every-BODY, with an island twist. No dance experience or coordination required.* This shy, awkward, high social anxiety and stage fright ridden little girl decided she was going to emerge from her shell. It wasn't something that I chose, it chose me; and I have to tell you, the energy from dancing with a bunch of other people who are all there to let it all go and 'dance with me in my room' is totally unparalleled. After I've finished teaching a class I am typically smiling from ear to ear, sweating like crazy, and so spiritually energized I am almost bouncing off the wall. The Bliss Buzz I am on after one of my classes usually lasts until my head hits the pillow at night!

Do you have a type of dance that leaves you feeling Bliss Buzzed?

Dance Is Profound

What is it about dancing? Most people enjoy dance in some form or another: traditional, social, fitness. Whether we are spectators or participants, most of us enjoy dance. It sparks something in us. What is that all about?

Dancing has a profound, sometimes underestimated, impact on our minds, bodies, and spirits. Sure, it's a lot of fun but there's more to it than that.

Benefits of Dance

According to Madeline Knight there are nine main benefits of dancing:

1. Boost Memory

Dance not only instills grace, but it also helps you age gracefully. According to a study in *The New England Journal of Medicine*, dancing may boost your memory and prevent you from developing dementia as you get older. Science reveals that aerobic exercise can reverse volume loss in the hippocampus, the part of the brain that controls memory. The hippocampus naturally shrinks during late adulthood, which often leads to impaired memory, and sometimes dementia.

2. Improve Flexibility

Those plies and arabesques that ballet dancers practice aren't just for aesthetics; they also increase flexibility, and reduce stiffness. You can skip the ballet slippers and still reap the benefits of ballet by practicing some simple stretches at home. Increasing your flexibility will help ease joint pain and post exercise soreness.

3. Reduce Stress

If you're feeling tense or stressed out, you might want to grab a partner, turn up the music, and tango! In a controlled study in the *Journal of Applied Gerontology*, researchers found that partner dance and musical accompaniment can help bring about stress relief.

4. Diminish Depression

Dancing really does lift your spirits, according to a study that tested the effects of dancing on people with depression. Patients who participated in an upbeat group dance showed the fewest depression symptoms and the most vitality. Got the blues? Grab a friend and go out dancing tonight.

5. Help Your Heart

Dance is a great activity for those at risk for cardiovascular disease. People with heart failure who took up waltzing improved their heart health, breathing, and quality of life significantly compared to those who biked or walked on a treadmill for exercise, noted an Italian study.

6. Lose Weight

Bored with your bicycle? A study in the *Journal of Physiological Anthropology* found that an exercise program of aerobic dance training is just as helpful for losing weight and increasing aerobic power as cycling and jogging.

7. Balance Better

If you are nervous about falling as you get older, some dance lessons might help ease your worries according to a study in the *Journal of Aging and Physical Activity* that showed tango dancing can improve balance in aging adults. Dancing requires a lot of fast movement and good posture, so frequent dancing will help you stabilize and gain better control of your body.

8. Increase Energy

Can't seem to find your get-up-and-go? Taking a dance class might help. Research published in *The Scholarly Publishing and Academic Resources Coalition* found that a weekly dance program could improve physical performance and increase energy levels among adults.

9. Make Friends

A dance class is the perfect setting to make new friends and branch out socially. Maintaining positive relationships may just rank up there with healthy eating and exercise. Being socially engaged leads to increased happiness, reduced stress, and a stronger immune system. [v]

What Does the Yogi Say?

Edane Padme, entrepreneur, yogi and my good friend, wrote in my Kelani Instructor Training manual an article about dancing, specifically the hips:

As humans, we connect with our environment through our bodies, our senses. When the movement of our bodies becomes one with the movement of our environment, we are touched by the richness and depth of our happiness. It is creative movement which touches our minds, bodies, and souls in the pursuit of ultimate health and wellness. Energy is meant to move, it is the living force within us. If you are having a hard time understanding "energy", simply rub your palms together while taking conscious deep breaths, after a minute bring your palms about two inches apart, you will feel a warm, tingling sensation. That is the energy flowing through us. It is our life force, chi, prana.

I read a quote that said, "Movement is the universal language of freedom." When we don't express our creativity we slowly die a spiritual death. We must liberate our souls by moving our energy within through dance, songs, poetry, and anything that moves you. Let go! Feel free, laugh, cry, sing, and feel every cell in your body dance. Physically, energy moves through the spine like two serpents, one flowing upward and the other flowing downward, spiraling around each other. When we don't move our hips, these energies stay within the root chakra.

The root chakra is the energy center of the genitals and reproductive system. The root chakra represents, ground, money, and sexuality.

When there is not enough energy in the root chakra, we may suffer from the loss of passion. The secret to living a healthy, energetic, balanced, and sacred lifestyle is to bring the energy through the chakras from the root to the crown chakra. This energy can be moved through Kelani, yoga and anything and everything that moves your hips. The rise of this energy from the root chakra to the crown chakra is a sacred experience. It is a mental orgasm, understanding. May we dance our way to Enlightenment![vi]

So whether you participate in a dance class, go out dancing with your friends, or simply shut the door to your room, blast your music and dance on your own, let the movement guide you to your Bliss Buzz!

3. Water Is My Yoga Mat

"Water is the central source of our beings. It is part of every cell and fiber in us; it is our very essence." Phylameana Lila Desy[vii]

Mmmm water. I have often contemplated the explanation behind the profound effect water has over every fiber of my being. Something happens to me when I am in the presence of water that I cannot put into words.

Let me give you a simple example. One morning at my friend's home, on a gorgeous sunny day, we took a walk through her massive backyard. She has a beautiful home right on the lake. As soon as I laid eyes on the water, I had the immediate sensation of overwhelming bliss wash over me (pun intended). It happens to me every single time I see, hear and touch water. In my mind, I compare the experience to a scene from a science fiction movie with a portal that sucks people into another dimension. This is the effect that water has on me, perhaps because of the deep-rooted connection I have to my South Pacific and Mediterranean ancestors.

I know I am not alone in how I feel. When so many of us imagine our ideal vacation we think of the beach, a lake, a pool, or a destination related to water. Why?

I did a lot of research and came across many ancient philosophies supporting this. The Taoist philosophy speaks in depth (yes, that is another pun) of water and its properties.

Bruce Lee used water in one of his powerful quotes:

"Don't get set into one form, adapt it and build your own, and let it grow, be like water. Empty your mind, be formless, shapeless – like water. Now you put water in a cup, it becomes a cup; you put water into a bottle, it becomes the bottle; you put it in a teapot, it becomes the teapot. Water can flow or it can crash. Be water, my friend." [viii]

Perhaps the most clear and simple explanation was what I read about one of the Buddhist values, which states that water symbolises purity, clarity, and calmness; and reminds us to cleanse our minds and attain the states of purity. [ix]

To me, part of the attraction stems from the fact that water is so calm and yet so unbelievably powerful. Like the yin and yang.

Phylameana Lila Desy writes:

Water is the central source of our beings. It is part of every cell and fiber in us; it is our very essence. Could water be the common denominator that weaves us all (earth, animal, human, and plant) together as one? Is it the ultimate connector? It's awesome and humbling that water carries so many entrained messages, especially when we consider that there has been the same water and the same amount of water on Earth for millions of years. [x]

The Man and the Sea

I interviewed someone who has a wealth of authority and knowledge on the subject of the sea. His name is Edmond and he is my dear father. A professional deep sea fisherman and deep sea diver of the Mediterranean Sea for most of his life, I feel his relationship with water has been deep (maybe we should start counting my puns) and profound on so many levels.

Upon interviewing my father, I asked what the sea meant to him. Not surprisingly, he had a lot to say. While I thought I knew everything about his relationship and adventures with the sea, there was a lot more that I learned. This is only part of what he told me:

While the sea can be a means of survival and can at times be unpredictable and unforgiving, it has also been a safe haven for him. Having gone through his fair share of hardships, the serenity of the ocean has been his sanctuary. Away from the noise and the cars, the hustle and bustle of his surroundings, and the hyper-stimulation of the world, being out there in the middle of the water is deeply therapeutic for him.

He says that when he takes his boat out, the air is so fresh, so clear, and so clean. He is in love with the tranquility of it all.

"No more people, no more cars, no more noise, no more talking."

As a child, I remember him filling up his oxygen tanks and getting all suited up for diving. He said to me that nothing compares to the tranquility that lies beneath the surface of the sea. As soon as your head plunges, all goes silent.

"You just forget yourself," my dad said. "The feeling of being under the water is completely another world. Peace is there when you are in the ocean. You feel the beauty of life and nature."

My dad amazes me to this very day. Pushing 70 and still as strong as an ox, with his tanned skin, his Popeye the Sailor biceps, and a core that could challenge even the most fit Pilates instructor, the sea and him are now, as they have always been, one entity. Water is not a hobby for him, it IS him.

Meditate on That

One summer my family and I were on a yacht in Florida. While everyone was inside the cabin, I sat outside on the bow of the yacht. My daughter asked, as I walked alongside to the front, "Mommy, why are you going to sit way at the front of the boat?" I explained to her that for me, this was the ultimate form of meditation. Every time the boat went flying through the air by a wave, then came crashing down, the salty water splashed all over my body. I loved every second of it! It felt exhilarating, magical, and therapeutic, pure bliss! Even after we docked on land, I walked around the rest of the day totally Bliss Buzzed from this simple experience of being bathed by the salty water in the wind.

On one of my favorite family vacations to date, we were in the South of France visiting a gorgeous location called Cap-d'Ail. It is a breathtaking body of water in the Mediterranean Sea, nestled in a valley. To get there you need to walk, and walk, and walk. We trekked with our kids down the side of the mountain to reach the beach and, oh my, it was worth it. It was nothing short of magical and spectacular.

I swam out into the sea and as I lay there, floating, staring up at the mountains and into the blue sky, I breathed in all that bliss. The profound energy was again, pure meditation.

I have so many other water Bliss Buzzes. Waterfalls in Samoa, the red sea in Jordan and Egypt, the South Pacific Ocean in New Zealand and the list goes on. Each of these moments has been my yoga mat.

While I would love to be back at any of those destinations, I am able to- in my very own home- recreate the exhilaration by simply recalling it: a.k.a. visualization. It is as easy as stepping into the shower or the bath, closing my eyes, and simply visualizing my blissful water retreats to recreate my Bliss Buzz.

Mmmm water...

4. Healing Hugs

Anyone who knows me will attest to the fact that I am a huge fan of hugging. There are many other fellow huggers out there. Maybe even you, person reading this book, is a hugger. What is our story? Is there a science behind our hug addiction?

I nursed (breastfed) all my daughters (in fact, I wrote most of this book while nursing my third daughter). I recall over the years reading about the importance of touch. If mothers were having problems breastfeeding their babies, experts recommended (and still do) 'mooning' or skin-to-skin contact. This would encourage the release of breast milk and help mom and baby in the process. One of the reasons, and this is still amazing to me, is that there is a mutual release of hormones between mother and baby which assists in the 'let down' or release of the milk. I remember being so amazed to learn that it was even possible for mothers of adopted babies to breastfeed their little ones. How amazing is that? It is all about the profound effects of touch.

At a conference I attended years ago, one of the presenters shared a study, which demonstrated that people with occupations that involve touch (such as massage therapists) actually live longer. This proves yet again the value of touch.

Studies show that human contact has many health benefits. The touch of loved ones increases hemoglobin in the blood, which helps our body increase oxygen flow throughout the body, including the heart and brain. Increased hemoglobin helps speed the healing process after illness. Hugging can help build a good immune system, decrease the risk of heart disease, and decrease levels of the stress hormone cortisol in women.

According to the American Psychosomatic Society, a hug or 10 minutes of holding hands with a romantic partner can help reduce stress, and its harmful physical effects.[xi]

So, the next time you see someone you have a connection with, give them a long hug and then, when you're done, hug them again. Then tell them it is for your mutual health and for the Bliss Buzz. In this case, it would be a double shot!

5. Vitamin S

"We all smile in the same language." Unknown

Don't forget your daily dose of vitamin S: the smile vitamin.

Something enlightening occurred during the summer of 2012 while my mother was going through cancer and chemotherapy treatment. I created a photo album on Facebook which initially served the purpose of sharing her journey with loved ones (especially my mother's nine siblings around the world) who wanted to be kept in the loop but could not be with her in person. Eventually, however, it turned into something more. The album became a source of inspiration to many others, especially from our local community. The album was named: *Granny Warrior Princess Cancer Journey – Diaries of a Family Going through the Cancer Journey with a Smile.*

In documenting her journey, we took countless pictures. To prepare for each picture we would pose, look at the picture to see if we liked it, and if we didn't, we would try to pose again: "Smile! Let's try that again. Smile again!" This process became hilarious and our smiles, usually selfies for the camera, turned into smiles, even hysterical laughter, off the camera. There was a shift of focus from the chemo drugs in her IV, to what angle made us look like we had one chin, not two.

Interestingly and not surprisingly (we discovered this much later) there are actual health benefits of smiling. Mark Stibich, Ph.D., wrote an article about the *Top 10 Reasons to Smile*. He says that smiling is a great way to make yourself stand out while helping your body to function better. *Smile to improve your health, your stress level, and your attractiveness. Smiling is just one fun way to live longer.*

Top 10 Reasons to Smile by **Mark Stibich, Ph.D.**

1. Smiling Makes Us Attractive

We are drawn to people who smile. There is an attraction factor. We want to know a smiling person and figure out what is so good. Frowns, scowls, and grimaces all push people away but a smile draws them in.

2. Smiling Changes Our Mood

Next time you are feeling down, try putting on a smile. There's a good chance your mood will change for the better. Smiling can trick the body into helping you change your mood.

3. Smiling Is Contagious

When someone is smiling they lighten up the room, change the moods of others, and make things happier. A smiling person brings happiness with them. Smile lots and you will draw people to you.

4. Smiling Relieves Stress

Stress can really show up in our faces. Smiling helps to prevent us from looking tired, worn down, and overwhelmed. When you are stressed, take time to put on a smile. The stress should be reduced and you'll be better able to take action.

5. Smiling Boosts Your Immune System

Smiling helps the immune system to work better. When you smile, immune function improves, possibly because you are more relaxed. Prevent the flu and colds by smiling.

6. Smiling Lowers Your Blood Pressure

When you smile, there is a measurable reduction in your blood pressure. Give it a try if you have a blood pressure monitor at home. Sit for a few minutes; take a reading. Then smile for a minute and take another reading while still smiling. Do you notice a difference?

7. Smiling Releases Endorphins, Natural Pain Killers and Serotonin

Studies have shown that smiling releases endorphins, natural painkillers, and serotonin. Together, these three make us feel good. Smiling is a natural drug.

8. Smiling Lifts the Face and Makes You Look Younger

The muscles we use to smile lift the face, making a person appear younger. Don't go for a face lift, just try smiling your way through the day; you'll look younger and feel better.

9. Smiling Makes You Seem Successful

Smiling people appear more confident, are more likely to be promoted, and are more likely to be approached. Put on a smile at meetings and appointments; people will react to you differently.

10. Smiling Helps You Stay Positive

Try this test: Smile. Now try to think of something negative without losing the smile. It's hard. When we smile our body is sending the rest of us a message that "Life is good!" Stay away from depression, stress, and worry by smiling. [xii]

And guess what? Smiling is free, so start smiling now! Enjoy the free Bliss Buzz of your vitamin S.

6. Karaoke Therapy

"Singing is cheaper than therapy, healthier than drinking, and certainly more fun than working out." Stacy Horn [xiii]

"A ship in port is safe but that's not what the ships are built for." John A. Shedd [xiv]

"Life begins at the end of your comfort zone." Neale Donald Walsch [xv].

Like many people, I love to sing. I am not a professional nor do I have the best technical voice, but it does not change the fact that I belt out a tune as passionately as a professional recording artist does.

Back in 2001, as I watched *American Idol* (the popular reality singing competition) on TV, I remember thinking how exciting but nerve wracking it must be to audition and be part of a show like that. I have always loved singing, but as most people, I used to stick to shower and car singing. I also had severe stage fright to the point where during my school and university days, I would have high anxiety and panic attacks any time I knew I would have to present a project or speech to my peers, or even speak in front of my peers. I was that person that would not ask questions, even if I were clueless, in order to avoid everyone looking at me. Moreover, I had all the typical stage fright symptoms: dry mouth, clammy hands, and shaky voice – you name it. It was paralyzing torture for me.

In 2001, I was working at a hotel assisting the general manager. He also taught hotel management courses at a college. One day he asked if I would take his place for the day to teach his class (having a degree in hotel management and having worked in the field for the better part of a decade, he figured I was qualified). I panicked and catapulted into high anxiety mode! I explained to him my extreme fear of public speaking. That day he had a long talk with me, encouraging me to step out of my box and comfort zone and just do it. There is a saying by Neale Donalde Walsch: "Life begins at the end of your comfort zone." [xvi] I get that, and to this day, I continue to do things on a regular basis that are outside my comfort zone, and feel as though I have grown every time I do. I did not end up teaching the class but the speech stuck with me.

In 2005, *Canadian Idol* (the Canadian version of American Idol) was born. 28 years old was the age cut-off age for auditioning. I was 28 years old. It was my last chance. I picked up my family and we drove to Kitchener and waited in line for maybe ten hours with my little daughter Leilani, who was about two years old at the time.

What was I doing? Nerves overcame me but there was no turning back. This was something I had to do.

I got in the room (actually, it was a trailer), stepped forward in front of three stoic judges, and sang. My mouth was dry, my voice was shaky, but I did not stop. I kept going. I did it.

There were about four of us auditioning in that trailer that day. After we were all done, we stood there and then received it: the "we hope you enjoyed your experience" speech, followed by "you did not make it through to the next round".

I walked out of the trailer, tail between my legs, back to my hotel room, and cried. I am not sure what I was expecting the outcome to be, but it certainly was not this. What a disaster right? Wrong! Despite the verdict, I did it. I did something that I never thought I would do. Was it difficult? Yes it was, beyond words. Was I saddened that I did not make it through? Yes, I was devastated. Would I change anything if I could go back in time? No, I absolutely would not change a thing.

So can you guess what I did next? I wiped my tears, picked myself back up, and announced to my husband that I wanted to audition again the following week in a different city. He was perplexed (to say the least). It was difficult for me to explain, but I had to give it one more shot. I pulled myself together, and between one week and another, I practiced singing at work (I worked at a gym at the time).

My manager would pull random gym members into the fitness studio and have me sing in front of them for practice. They would give me their opinions, and with every practice round, I stepped further out of my comfort zone and not only broke through, but broke down some walls that had been living inside of me all my life.

The next week auditions were in Toronto, and there I was, in line at the crack of dawn. I waited, but not as long this time.

I walked in the room, again with about three other contestants. I sang, took a step back, and waited for the others in the room to audition. The judges then asked a couple of them to leave the room and asked me and another girl to stay behind so we could sing another song! They liked me! I sang again, this time a different song. The judges told me my voice was pretty but that it was not what they were looking for. I did not make it past that point that day, but I did walk out exhilarated, elated, so proud of myself, and unbelievably Bliss Buzzed.

I did it.

This experience was better than the last because stepping out of my comfort zone during the first audition broadened my horizons. That buzz lasted with me for such a long time. I had done it! I stepped out of my comfort zone and it paid off! I will never be able to say I did not give it a shot. I tried. Every time we push our own boundaries, the fear, the nerves, the dry mouth, the sweaty palms, the shaking – those are all signs that we are so unequivocally alive in that moment. And once we do it, we are exhilarated to a point we cannot even explain.

I got hooked. My husband was perplexed. He thought I was a glutton for punishment. Why would someone keep on trying out only to be rejected time and time again, and then go back for more? But that's just it, it isn't about winning or losing, it's about the experience and the sheer love of singing.

Benefits of Singing

Group singing is cheaper than therapy, healthier than drinking and certainly more fun than working out. It is the one thing in life where feeling better is almost a guarantee.

There are many benefits of singing: physical, emotional, and social.

Physically

1. Singing exercises our lungs. It tones up our intercostal muscles and our diaphragm.
2. It can improve our sleep.
3. We benefit our hearts and circulation by improving our aerobic capacity and we decrease muscle tension.
4. Our facial muscles get toned.
5. Our posture improves.
6. We can become more mentally alert.
7. Sinuses and respiratory tubes are opened up more.
8. With careful training, recent evidence suggests that it can help decrease the problem of snoring.
9. There is a release of pain relieving endorphins.
10. Our immune system is given a boost enabling us to fight disease.
11. It can help reduce anger and depression and anxiety.

12. Use of music can help people to regain balance if affected by illness such as Parkinson's disease.

Emotionally

1. Increase in self-esteem and confidence.
2. It increases feelings of wellbeing.
3. It enhances mood.
4. Useful as a stress reducer.
5. It is uplifting spiritually
6. It can increase positive feelings.
7. Encourages creativity.
8. It can be energizing.
9. It evokes emotions.
10. Promotes bonding.
11. Increases understanding and empathy between cultures.
12. It is healing.

Socially

1. It enables you to meet more people.
2. Is a forum for sharing.
3. Brings people together and encourages a sense of community.
4. Offers opportunity for giving and receiving positive feedback.
5. A forum for fun and laughter.
6. Support.
7. Provides a safe environment to try new skills.
8. Brings people together.

Give It a Try!

Life-Affirming Benefits of Singing – Vocalizing Promotes Well Being by Patty Mills:

Singing fortifies health, widens culture, refines the intelligence, enriches the imagination, makes for happiness and endows life with an added zest.

If you sing in the shower or sing along with the radio, consider taking this raw vocal skill to new heights. Music, the "universal language", not only stirs our deepest emotions, but active participation can increase energy and vigor to see us through even the most stress-filled life commitments. Good vocal technique goes beyond the basics to include both physical and vocal warm-ups, proper nutrition, adequate rest, and emotional commitment. An experienced vocal teacher will explore all aspects of posture, abdominal and chest development, tone production, and breath control. What health club can promise these benefits?

- Singing increases poise, self-esteem, and presentation skills.
- Singing strengthens concentration and memory.
- Singing develops the lungs and promotes superior posture.
- Singing broadens expressive communication.
- Singing adds a rich, more pleasant quality to speech.
- Singing animates the body, mind, and spirit.
- Singing enables the performer to delve into acting/characterization.
- Singing stimulates insight into prose and poetry and piques interests in the inner meaning of words.

- Singing enriches one's ability to appreciate the art of great singers.
- Singing is an ageless enjoyment; you are never too young or too old.
- Singing is therapeutic both emotionally and physically.[xvii]

Singing Is Good for You

Not only is singing a great way to raise money, research shows that it's also good for your heart.

Professor Graham Welch, Chair of Music Education at the Institute of Education, University of London, has studied developmental and medical aspects of singing for 30 years. He says the health benefits of singing are both physical and psychological. *Singing has physical benefits because it is an aerobic activity that increases oxygenation in the blood stream and exercises major muscle groups in the upper body, even when sitting. Singing has psychological benefits because of its normally positive effect in reducing stress levels through the action of the endocrine system which is linked to our sense of emotional well-being. Psychological benefits are also evident when people sing together as well as alone because of the increased sense of community, belonging and shared endeavour.*

All for One Choir also advocates the importance of singing to help keep your heart healthy. Choir members sang for their hearts when they performed a flash mob in Princes Quay Shopping Centre in Hull.

Regular exercising of the vocal cords can even prolong life, according to research done by leading vocal coach and singer Helen Astrid, from The Helen Astrid Singing Academy in London. *It's a great way to keep in shape because you are exercising your lungs and heart. Not only that, your body produces 'feel good' hormones called endorphins, which rush around your body when you sing. It's exactly the same when you eat a bar of chocolate. The good news with singing is that you don't gain any calories!*

Singing even helps you live longer according to the findings of a joint Harvard and Yale study, which showed that choral singing increased the life expectancy of the population of New Haven, Connecticut. The report concluded that this was because singing promoted both a healthy heart and an enhanced mental state. Another study at the University of California has reported higher levels of immune system proteins in the saliva of choristers after performing a complex Beethoven masterwork.

Bjorn Vickhoff who led a study at the University of Gothenburg in Sweden into music and wellbeing, also believes that singing has positive effects on your health. The study showed how musical structure influenced the heart rate of choir members. *Singing is good for your health. Our research indicates that it may even be good for your heart. Further research in this field is much needed, such as the long-term effect of choir singing.*

So go on, keep your heart healthy and get singing![xviii]

My husband gets it now.

Since then I have auditioned for *Canada's Got Talent* (national televised talent show), entered a local karaoke competition three years in a row, and one year I actually made it to the finals of a competition known as *Rose City Rockstar!* I sang onstage at the Caesar's Palace Casino. I-Ioana- the person who did not even want to raise her hand in class in grade school, did all this. To this day it boggles my mind.

Fast forward to today. Mark my words that if there is a karaoke machine, a stage, and a microphone, then I will be up there singing my heart out. I may be nervous and clammy right before I get on, but I will totally be getting my Bliss Buzz on stage which will linger with me for days and days on end.

7. Community

One of the many things I loved about having my own Pilates and dance studio (Studio Kelani) was our community. When I speak of holistic wellness I always say that you can eat 'perfectly' and workout until you are blue in the face, but if your spirit is not well, then unfortunately, you are not in perfect health.

A vital component of the spirit and holistic health, in my humble opinion, is community. People may underestimate this value but the studies are clear.

People all over the world gather, as an example, on Holy days whether it be Churches, Mosques, Synagogues, Ashrams, Temples, etc. on a regular basis, and after engaging in Prayer, many stay on to engage in communal events.

It seems to me however, that these practices are becoming fewer and far between. Where in the past people in the Western world did not work on Sundays, now, in a world fuelled by a consumer driven mentality, Sunday is yet another go-go-go-busy-busy-rush-rush day. Big box grocery stores are flooded with people stocking up in a 'here comes the apocalypse' way, purchasing oversized quantities of everything they need and then piling them onto a mountain of things they want. Unfortunately, people do not realize how important a 'stop' day is; how important these community type events, religious or otherwise, really are. Studies show that people engaged in community life actually live longer. The younger generation benefits from the older generation and vice versa.

I love big family gatherings. I know for myself that when I am at a large family gathering and there is the buzz of kids running around; people gathered in the kitchen; around a campfire; or around a pool, I absolutely love it. It totally gives me a Bliss Buzz.

Sadly though, I find that with the advancing (I use the word loosely) of technology, specifically social media, we are the most connected and disconnected we have ever been. While social sites like Facebook (don't get me wrong, I am an avid user of Facebook) create online communities, it seems the opposite holds true of the real world. Social networks are fine, until we start to confuse them, or worse yet, use them as replacements for our real life communities.

Perhaps if we had more community life we would not need as many support groups.

We text, e-mail, Facebook message, tweet, but rarely pick up the phone or, dare I say it, engage in live interactions.

I make it a point to meet with my friends every so often, even if it's for a quick breakfast or tea at arbitrary times. We don't have to wait until a Friday night. It may be for an hour or fifteen minutes. When I have had a great live conversation, I leave feeling inspired, and energized, and totally Bliss Buzzed! It does not take much. And when I get that buzz it stays with me for hours and hours until I get my next 'hit'.

8. I Kid You Not

"We don't stop playing because we grow up, we grow up because we stop playing." George Bernard Shaw[xix]

Have you ever had a conversation with a child? Children are amazing. I am always fascinated by children's points of view. Just like the show *Kids Say the Darnedest Things* suggests, children absolutely do say the most amazing things! They are hilarious and enlightening.

I have three children: 11 years old, 8 years old and 18 months old. The things that come out of their mouths never cease to amuse and amaze me. They are refreshingly innocent, honest, not jaded, with wild and beautiful imaginations.

One day, as we walked into a hotel, my 8 year old daughter Keona, who was seven years old at the time, stopped and said, "Look mommy, there's an owl up there." I was confused. I looked up and sure enough, there was a fake owl at the entrance of the hotel, above the doorway. It seemed random to me until I later discovered that owls are used to keep rats away. Had my daughter not pointed it out to me, I likely would not have even noticed it or learned that fact. Thank you Keona!

I find their observations fantastic. My kids, as with the owl story, are constantly pointing out things that I otherwise would not have seen. The beautiful pattern on a stone from the beach, the images the clouds in the sky resemble, and so on. Everything is so exciting to them. It reminds me of the music video of a child sitting in a car with both hands spread out of the window, and her bright eyes wide open gazing out as the world goes by, awestruck by everything.

Somewhere during the course of growing up many adults lose that, maybe because of life experiences; stress; the weight of our responsibilities; circumstances such as illness, trauma and death? So much can cause us to become jaded and create layer, upon layer, upon layer, which inadvertently changes the way we see (or do not see) everything. Nevertheless, I do not think that it is impossible for us to recall that ability, to retrain ourselves back to the simplicity of it all, to peel off the layers from our eyes, to strip back down to that beautiful gift of innocence and appreciation of the simple things we are all born with. It's not that complicated. In fact, the beauty is in the de-complication (and yes, I did make up that word). Children help us get back there.

I have traveled to so many countries with my children. In fact, to date, my two oldest Leilani and Keona have visited ten countries (Mahniya needs to catch up as she is only at two so far), and what I can say with sincerity and certainty is that the wealth of experience from each trip has been magnified because of them.

There is a study done by the author of the book *Blue Zones* which shows that one of the factors leading to a long, healthy life, is the importance of children to seniors (and vice versa). Therefore, children are, without a doubt, healing. [xx]

So the next time you are feeling jaded, sit with a child and just chat. I bet you will have a bunch of Bliss Buzz moments!

9. Give a Little

"As you grow older you will discover you have two hands, one for helping yourself, the other for helping others." Audrey Hepburn[xxi]

"You must be the change you wish to see in the world." Mahatma Ghandi[xxii]

We live in an age where globalization has made us more aware of our fellow humans and the issues that affect us. This includes bad news, which there is all too much of including war, illness and poverty. Sometimes we do not need to travel far as these problems can be in our back yards, or even our own homes. Issues like these leave us feeling sad and oftentimes, helpless. But there is hope. Organizations were created for the benefit not only of those who are in need, but for those of us who want to help. There are countless opportunities for us to make a difference.

I remember watching an episode of the sitcom *Friends*, and one of the characters, Phoebe, tried to find a completely selfless act to undertake. She had such a hard time though because even selfless acts made her feel good, thereby- in her mind- negating the selflessness factor. There is something to be said about that. The same holds true of volunteering your time for a good cause. When you volunteer your time selflessly, purely out of the goodness of your heart, expecting absolutely nothing in return, it is really a fantastic and rewarding feeling. Studies demonstrate that those who volunteer their time for a good cause are more likely to live longer than those who do not.[xxiii] Studies also show that those who derive more joy out of doing things for other people than deriving joy from acquiring material possessions are generally happier overall. It is a win-win situation![xxiv]

When I lived in Windsor (Ontario, Canada), I was part of the warm-up for three years in a row of one of one of Canada's largest nation-wide fundraising campaigns called the CIBC Run for the Cure. During the second and third year, this resonated with me even more as my mom was fighting and then recovering from breast cancer. Without exception, every year I stood onstage and peered out into the sea of those thousands of people decked out in pink and white, I was overwhelmed with emotion. There is something profound about a mass of people gathering for a good cause. The energy was tangible and moving. At that one moment in time, it did not matter where you were from, what size or color you were or what race or religion you belonged to. Everyone was there for one cause and one cause alone – to make a positive difference. It was such an honor to be part of something so moving.

After I was done with the warm-up and cool down for all those people, the feeling of elation and warmth and Bliss Buzz lingered with me for so long.

The act of giving is a gift in itself. I try to instil that in my children. In 2014, my children, on Christmas Eve and in the spirit of giving, donated their long locks to kids with cancer. That was my gift to them, to experience the joy that comes from a selfless act. They were so excited.

Over the years, my children and I have initiated and volunteered at countless fundraisers. There is no gift more precious than the gift of giving.

The next time you have the opportunity to volunteer some of your time, or do some good for your community, or for society in general, I am confident that doing it will give you a warm Bliss Buzz!

10. Food Glorious Food

"Nutrition is not low fat. It's not low calorie. It's not being hungry and feeling deprived. It's nourishing your body with real, whole foods so that you are consistently satisfied and energized to live life to the fullest." Dietician Cassie[xxv]

When I was in grade school, I played the role of Mrs. Bumble in the theatrical production of Oliver Twist. The lyrics to the song Food Glorious Food echo in my ears to this day: *Food, glorious food! What wouldn't we give for, That extra bit more --That's all that we live for, Why should we be fated to, Do nothing but brood, On food, Magical food, Wonderful food, Marvellous food, Fabulous food.* [xxvi]

At the time, I resented that role because Mrs. Bumble was a mean old woman who was not in the best shape of her life, and as I was a chubby little girl, perhaps on some level, I felt they chose me for that reason. It has taken me 37 years, and years of battling eating disorders for me to finally not only admit but embrace my love of food. I am a self-professed foodie, and that's ok.

For centuries, food has brought people together. It is a communal act, which is one of the common denominators in all religions, groups, beliefs in the world. When people come together in celebration, they eat. When they come together to mourn, they eat. When they come together to meet for business, they eat. It is not a wonder, then, that there is an emotional attachment to food. It has been passed down from generation to generation. There is therefore no need to feel bad if you are one of the billions around the world who have linked food to some kind of emotion. The good news is, this can be used to our advantage! The trick is to eat the right kind of food.

Different kinds of food can stimulate different parts of the body, specifically the brain. There is a reason we enjoy chocolate so much. Chocolate actually triggers the brain to release endorphins, the feel good chemical. Cheese has that same effect. If we choose foods that are clean and high in nutritional value, they can stimulate all the correct responses in our body and actually make us happy. It's no secret that when we eat unhealthy food we feel unhealthy, and the same concept holds true of healthy food. As soon as we are at a place in our lives that we realize the importance of, and then adopt, the mind frame and mentality of getting excited about eating, we are already on the right track. Then after you've had a "live" meal full of enzymes, minerals and vitamins, you literally feel like you are buzzed. It is a true state of Bliss Buzzing. In the following article by Maya Dangerfield, there are 10 nutrients which are specifically proven to make us feel awesome! Enjoy:

Want some pep in your step? Perhaps a dash of good cheer (who doesn't, right)? Look no further than the grocery store's shelves. Foods rich in vitamins, minerals, and fatty acids are not only super healthy, but can also increase happiness, lessen symptoms of depression, and quell anxiety.

How can foods improve our moods? It all comes down to the brain. A healthy cognitive system is essential to regulating mood, and certain nutrients have a profound impact on maintaining normal brain function. To date, researchers have studied the association between foods and the brain and identified nine nutrients that can combat depression and boost our mood: calcium, chromium, folate, iron, magnesium, omega-3 fatty acids, vitamin B6, vitamin B12, vitamin D, and zinc. Try one of these foods for a mid-day pick-me-up, to promote long-term happiness, or to ward off the nagging worry that you forgot to lock the front door. (You did remember, right?)

1. Calcium

The most abundant mineral in the body, calcium plays an important role in maintaining strong bones and healthy blood vessels, and in reducing the risk of Type 2 diabetes. Low levels of calcium may play a role in PMS-related depression in particular. (Sorry guys, we couldn't find data on whether calcium can also regulate male fluctuations in mood.) Calcium deficiency affects more women than men, so women should take special care to meet the daily requirements.

How eating it helps: Found in a variety of sources (non-dairy included), calcium is often paired with vitamin D to help regulate mood fluctuations attributed to PMS. Since estrogen plays a large role in calcium production, calcium consumption may improve PMS-related depression.

2. Chromium

A trace mineral found in small amounts in the body, chromium helps the body metabolize food. A lack of chromium hurts the body's ability to regulate insulin (the hormone that regulates sugar) and may lead to diabetes-related complications like vision loss and high blood pressure.

How eating it helps: Chromium plays an important role in increasing the brain's level of serotonin, norepinephrine, and melatonin, which help the brain regulate emotion and mood. Because chromium works directly with the brain's mood regulators, it's been found to be an effective treatment of depression.

3. Folate

Folate (alternatively known as B9 or folic acid) helps the body create new cells and supports serotonin regulation. Serotonin passes messages between nerve cells and helps the brain manage a variety of functions, from determining mood to regulating social behavior. Folate deficiency can cause fatigue in addition to lowering levels of serotonin.

How eating it helps: A pair of power nutrients, Folate and B12 are often paired together to treat depression. By itself, Folate has the added benefit of boosting the efficiency of antidepressants.

4. Iron

Iron plays an important role in the body, from transporting oxygen to supporting energy levels and aiding muscle strength. Low levels of iron can lead to feelings of fatigue and depression. Iron deficiency appears more frequently in women than men, especially women of childbearing age.

How eating helps: Consuming enough iron will help prevent iron anemia (not enough iron), a condition that commonly affects women more than men. Keeping enough iron in the body is important, as the fatigue, apathy, and mood change associated with the iron deficiency can often lead to depression.

5. Magnesium

Magnesium is a mineral that plays over 300 roles in maintaining and protecting the body's health. Deficiency can cause irritability, fatigue, mental confusion, and predisposition to stress.

How eating it helps: Magnesium plays a large role in the development of serotonin, which is a major contributor to feelings of happiness. Due to its ability to help regulate emotions, it's a common element in homeopathic remedies for balancing mood.

6. Omega-3s

Omega-3 is an essential fatty acid that plays an important role in brain health and contributes up to 18 percent of the brain's weight. The body does not naturally produce Omega-3s, so the fatty acid needs to be consumed from outside sources. Deficiency symptoms include fatigue, mood swings, memory decline, and depression.

How eating it helps: Studies show a correlation between consumption of fish with high levels of Omega-3 fatty acids and a decreased risk of depression and suicide. Whether eating fish or snacking on chia seeds, increasing your intake of omega 3 fatty acids may help combat depression.

7. Vitamin B6

Vitamin B6 helps the production of neurotransmitters (which send messages from the brain to the rest of the body). Deficiency in B6 can cause short-term anemia; long-term effects include a weakened immune system, confusion, and depression.

How eating it helps: Consuming vitamin B6 is essential for regulating brain function, which influences our emotions. In addition to regulating healthy moods, vitamin B6 is also an effective method for treating premenstrual depression.

8. Vitamin B12

B12 is an essential element that aids in the creation of red blood cells and nerves. Low levels of B12 can cause short-term fatigue, slowed reasoning, and paranoia, and are associated with depression. Vitamin B12 is found naturally in meats, eggs, and animal by-products, meaning vegetarians and vegans have an increased risk of developing a deficiency.

How eating it helps: Because moods depend largely on signals from the brain, B12 plays an important role in regulating depression. Consuming enough vitamin B12 allows the body to synthesize a group of nutrients critical for normal neurological function.

9. Vitamin D

Vitamin D helps regulate cell growth, plays an important role in maintaining the immune system, and (when paired with calcium) protects bones. Studies show that low levels of vitamin D are associated with depressive symptoms in both men and women. Most often, lowered levels of vitamin D are the result of indoor lifestyles, limited sun exposure, and inadequate intake of vitamin-D-rich foods.

How eating it helps: If you're feeling blue, increasing vitamin D could help ward off depression. Consuming the mood-regulating vitamin is important, especially during the wintertime when light from the sun (a natural producer of vitamin D) is limited.

10. Zinc

Zinc is found in almost every cell and plays an important role in supporting a healthy immune system and helping the body protect the gut from damage. Low levels of zinc in the diet can lead to a variety of ailments, including a weakened immune system, loss of appetite, anemia, hair loss, and depression. Vegetarians need as much as 50 percent more zinc than non-vegetarians due to the body's lower absorption rate of plant-based zinc.

How eating it helps: Studies have identified zinc as an important factor in decreasing depressive symptoms, as the vitamin can improve the response of antidepressants while reducing the side effects of anti-depression medication. A lack of zinc can trigger depressive behaviors, so load up on zinc-rich foods to balance your mood.[xxvii]

The bottom line is that food can be your friend, not your enemy, and your ultimate source of a Bliss Buzz!

11. Barefooting

"If you're not barefoot then you're overdressed." Unknown.

Barefooting? I bet you did not think it was an actual word did you? Barefooting is actually a 'movement' (pun intended) and has become fairly popular.

For as long as I can remember I have always loved being barefoot. When we lived on the island of Samoa (my mother's home island), we were not allowed to wear shoes in the classroom. Brilliant! I live in Canada now, and for as much as I can get away with it, I am barefoot. I am often asked, especially when I get on cold concrete surfaces in the non-summer times of the year, "Aren't your feet freezing?" and my answer is always the same, "I'm always barefoot so I'm used to it." In fact, I clearly remember when working at a gym where sneakers were mandatory that I could not wait to get into the studio to kick off my shoes to teach my classes. A couple of years back I was happy to discover that not only are there others out there like me, but that there is an actual 'barefoot movement' and increasing studies presenting the benefits of being barefoot. Of course, this all made perfect sense to me and I was tickled to see the evidence, which back up my lifestyle.

The Urban Dictionary defines barefooting as: *The practice of willingly and consistently walking without footwear of any kind, mostly outdoors, or in everyday life, as a sporting activity, to improve health conditions of feet, ankles, legs, circulatory and immune system, and mood, or as a fashion statement, just for pleasure, or even as a whole philosophy of life. There are several groups of individuals fond of barefooting, promoting all over the world this activity and striving to remove the almost ubiquitous biases about barefooting: commonly regarded as hazardous, unhealthy or unacceptable upon written or non-written dress codes, to gain tolerance for this lifestyle, spread the consciousness about the benefits of barefooting and make adepts*[xxviii].

Dr. Mercola published the following article titled: *Grounding: The Potent Antioxidant That Few Know about...and It's Free.*

While still in the vast minority, an increasing number of people are joining the barefoot running trend, throwing their shoes to the wind and letting their feet run free, literally.

In the modern world, it might sound "extreme" to give up your shoes, particularly when engaging in an activity as hard on your feet as running, but surrounding your feet with thick cushioning and stiff supports is actually the "new" trend, evolutionarily speaking.

Humans Went Without Running Shoes for Millions of Years.

Writing in the journal *Nature*, Harvard researchers explained:

Humans have engaged in endurance running for millions of years, but the modern running shoe was not invented until the 1970s. For most of human evolutionary history, runners were either barefoot or wore minimal footwear such as sandals or moccasins with smaller heels and little cushioning relative to modern running shoes.

Let's face it, your feet were designed to work without shoes. And while running barefoot does pose certain unique hazards, such as stepping on a sharp object or injuring your skin on abrasive pavement, there are reports that barefoot running is actually quite beneficial.

While the research is still limited and many of the reports anecdotal, running barefoot may actually decrease the likelihood of ankle sprains and chronic injuries.

Shoes Alter Your Gait, but is This Good or Bad?

Walking or running *with* shoes is quite a different experience than doing so *without* them. This is evidenced perhaps no more clearly than among children, who in the developed world, are virtually the only ones who have not yet grown accustomed to wearing shoes, and as such their gait should be more or less the way nature intended.

Indeed, research published in the *Journal of Foot and Ankle Research* revealed:

Shoes affect the gait of children. With shoes, children walk faster by taking longer steps with greater ankle and knee motion, and increased tibialis anterior activity. Shoes reduce foot motion and increase the support phases of the gait cycle.

During running, shoes reduce swing phase leg speed, attenuate some shock and encourage a rear foot strike pattern. The long-term effect of these changes on growth and development are currently unknown.

And therein lies the question: is footwear a boon or a bust to mankind? Surprising as it may sound, emerging research suggests modern running shoes, with their heavily cushioned, elevated heels, may actually encourage runners to strike the ground with their heel first, a move that generates a greater collision force with the ground, leading to an increased potential for injury. The Harvard researchers continued in *Nature*:

Here we show that habitually barefoot endurance runners often land on the fore-foot (fore-foot strike) before bringing down the heel, but they sometimes land with a flat foot (mid-foot strike) or, less often, on the heel (rear-foot strike). In contrast, habitually shod runners mostly rear-foot strike, facilitated by the elevated and cushioned heel of the modern running shoe.

Kinematic and kinetic analyses show that even on hard surfaces, barefoot runners who fore-foot strike generate smaller collision forces than shod rear-foot strikers. This difference results primarily from a more plantar flexed foot at landing and more ankle compliance during impact, decreasing the effective mass of the body that collides with the ground. Fore-foot and mid-foot-strike gaits were probably more common when humans ran barefoot or in minimal shoes, and may protect the feet and lower limbs from some of the impact-related injuries now experienced by a high percentage of runners.

This may explain how marathon runners in Kenya are able to run great distances barefoot with virtually no pain or injuries. Likewise, research reviewed by Michael Warburton, a physical therapist in Australia, revealed:

- Running-related chronic injuries to bone and connective tissue in the legs are rare in developing countries, where most people are habitually barefooted.

- Where barefoot and shod populations co-exist, as in Haiti, injury rates of the lower extremity are substantially higher in the shod population.

- Wearing footwear actually increases the likelihood of ankle sprains, one of the most common sports injuries, because it either decreases your awareness of foot position or increases the twisting torque on your ankle during a stumble.

- One of the most common chronic injuries in runners, planter fasciitis (an inflammation of the ligament running along the sole of your foot), is rare in barefoot populations.

- Running in bare feet reduces oxygen consumption by a few percent.

Grounding: The Overlooked Benefit of Going Barefoot

While much of the debate between the barefoot and the shoed-foot focuses on the potential for injury, another often-overlooked aspect is grounding. The technique of grounding, also known as earthing, is simple: you walk barefoot to "ground" with the earth. The scientific theory behind the health benefits seen from this simple practice is that your body absorbs negative electrons from the earth through the soles of your feet.

The earth is negatively charged, so when you ground, you're connecting your body to a negatively charged supply of energy. And since the earth has a greater negative charge than your body, you end up absorbing electrons from it. The grounding effect is, in my understanding, one of the most potent antioxidants we know of and may have an anti-inflammatory effect on your body. As written in the *Journal of Alternative and Complementary Medicine*:

It is well established, though not widely known, that the surface of the Earth possesses a limitless and continuously renewed supply of free or mobile electrons as a consequence of a global atmospheric electron circuit. Wearing shoes with insulating soles and/or sleeping in beds that are isolated from the electrical ground plane of the earth have disconnected most people from the earth's electrical rhythms and free electrons.

A previous study demonstrated that connecting the human body to the earth during sleep (earthing) normalizes the daily cortisol rhythm and improves sleep. A variety of other benefits were reported, including reductions in pain and inflammation. Subsequent studies have confirmed these earlier findings and documented virtually immediate physiological and clinical effects of grounding or earthing the body.

Unfortunately, few people ever walk barefoot anymore to experience the benefits of grounding. But it is very plausible that some of the people who have converted to barefoot running are experiencing benefits not only from the lack of shoes, but also from the increased connection to the earth.

Walking Barefoot Is a Valuable Aspect of a Healthy Lifestyle

Exercising barefoot outdoors is one of the most wonderful, inexpensive and powerful ways of incorporating earthing into your daily life and will also help speed up tissue repair, as well as easing the muscle pain you sometimes get from strenuous exercise. A review of the available research, published January 2012 in the *Journal of Environmental and Public Health*, agrees with the concept of reaping health benefits when connecting to the earth. According to the authors:

Mounting evidence suggests that the earth's negative potential can create a stable internal bioelectrical environment for the normal functioning of all body systems. Moreover, oscillations of the intensity of the earth's potential may be important for setting the biological clocks regulating diurnal body rhythms, such as cortisol secretion.

It is also well established that electrons from antioxidant molecules neutralize reactive oxygen species (ROS, or in popular terms, free radicals) involved in the body's immune and inflammatory responses. The National Library of Medicine's online resource PubMed lists 7021 studies and 522 review articles from a search of "antioxidant + electron + free radical." It is assumed that the influx of free electrons absorbed into the body through direct contact with the earth likely neutralize ROS and thereby reduce acute and chronic inflammation.

Throughout history, humans mostly walked barefoot or with footwear made of animal skins. They slept on the ground or on skins. Through direct contact or through perspiration-moistened animal skins used as footwear or sleeping mats, the ground's abundant free electrons were able to enter the body, which is electrically conductive. Through this mechanism, every part of the body could equilibrate with the electrical potential of the earth, thereby stabilizing the electrical environment of all organs, tissues, and cells.

Modern lifestyle has increasingly separated humans from the primordial flow of Earth's electrons. For example, since the 1960s, we have increasingly worn insulating rubber or plastic soled shoes, instead of the traditional leather fashioned from hides. Rossi has lamented that the use of insulating materials in post-World War II shoes has separated us from the Earth's energy field. Obviously, we no longer sleep on the ground as we did in times past.

During recent decades, chronic illness, immune disorders, and inflammatory diseases have increased dramatically, and some researchers have cited environmental factors as the cause. However, the possibility of modern disconnection with the Earth's surface as a cause has not been considered. Much of the research reviewed in this paper points in that direction.

When indoors, using a grounding pad or sheet is an excellent way to lower your risk of cardiovascular disease and other problems, such as carpal tunnel syndrome and tendonitis.

Before You Take off Your Shoes

Just taking off your shoes, if you've been wearing them all your life, does not mean you'll immediately attain proper barefoot running form. Many new barefoot runners continue to land heavily on their heels and the result can be injury. So if you decide to give barefoot running a try, make sure you do it slowly, progressing gradually to more and more time spent without shoes. A good starting point is to first try walking barefoot and then begin with quarter-mile barefoot runs.

Keep in mind also that your gait will be different than it is with your shoes on; this is expected. Listen to your body and try to tune in to your innate knowledge of how to run and walk barefoot. Allow your feet, ankles, knees, and hips to naturally change position in response to the terrain.

When you start going barefoot, it is best to initiate on naturally softer ground like grass, dirt paths and sand; not cement, asphalt, or hardwood. When the muscles and joints of your foot become more stable and the skin on the bottom of your feet thickens, you will be able to handle progressively more time barefoot and on a wider variety of surfaces.

While there are a growing number of minimalist footwear options now on the market that are designed to simulate barefoot running, some argue that these shoes are merely marketing ploys, and in fact, still change your gait from the way nature intended. Personally, I have tried one version that I liked very much and would recommend highly; although, since I traded in running for Peak Fitness, I haven't actually used them for runs.

One final note, barefoot running or walking doesn't have to be an all or nothing decision. You can incorporate as much barefoot time into your life as you feel comfortable with. Quite possibly, you'll enjoy it so much that you will naturally find yourself kicking off your shoes as much as possible.[xxix]

The Barefoot Guy

A few months ago, I became 'virtually' acquainted with someone via social media who goes by the name or Instagram handle @Just.Live.Barefoot. This person, Olivier Bertrand, is a true barefooter, walking the streets of France with his bare feet. Although I consider myself as somewhat of a barefooter, I do still wear shoes when I am out and about, shopping, driving etc. Olivier- however-travels everywhere in bare feet.

Intrigued by his lifestyle, I asked Olivier to tell me a little bit about what barefooting means to him. This is what he said (translated from French to English):

Walking barefoot is certainly one of the most natural things. Many of us like to be barefoot at home or in natural places like the garden, parks, beaches, or countryside. The preconceptions that we have of city living are such that we cannot imagine ourselves to be safe while barefooted.

The feet are the part of the body upon which our relationship with the earth is based. All the nerve endings are in the feet, and regardless of what one wears on their feet, the sensations and pleasures of walking barefoot are irreplaceable.

Also, when walking barefoot, we project a positive image of a free, relaxed, serene, and sensual person. The looks that people who are conscious of the benefits of walking barefoot give you reflect their support, respect, and encouragement. Often it makes some of them emulate you and some even indulge by removing their own shoes.

To varying degrees, all of us like to go barefooted and what is different is only the way to assume and assert ourselves as barefoot supporters or not. Sometimes our work allows us to fully experience this state of mind, but it is mostly not possible. The artistic community is much more conducive to certain legitimate freedoms than the rigid three-piece suits professional world. That may be why there are many going barefoot among musicians, actors, models...

All human beings aspire to move comfortably; too often physical comfort has been equated with the idea of material comfort. For a long time, walking with bare feet meant that you were poor and could not afford to pay for shoes, and it was a means to distinguish between classes. This idea still persists somewhat, yet most people unconsciously feel the real reasons that led them to go barefoot as much as they feel the need to break free without really knowing why.

It is important to know that the image conveyed by going barefoot is a positive image, contrary to perceived ideas. The reactions are almost always complicit. In very few cases, the reaction is mockery, which is always a psychological defense for not being able to understand what others understand.

Going barefooted is a comfort and a pleasure, not a religion. It is also to have an enviable attitude of all who exude a positive vision of what we are as human beings.

The first question that arises when one is barefoot concerns the dangers, particularly those city-based hazards. This is a major factor (after those psychological) that keeps people from removing their shoes. In most cases, these factors are unconscious pretexts that justify wearing shoes without having to face the reality of moral barriers. We must be clear on this: unless completely hypochondriac - and that has nothing to do with going barefoot - there is no particular danger other than what everyone encounters in their daily lives. You can get hurt in so many circumstances. Are our feet more likely to get hurt than anything else? And frankly, is a small cut serious enough nowadays to deny us the satisfaction to feel the ground beneath our feet? Nothing prevents us from having a small bottle of disinfectant, barefooted or not. We can injure our arms, hands or legs; does that mean we need to wear armor? Must we constantly guard against everything, despite the fact that our body contains incredible resources to make us to operate? Is it not wiser to trust our physiology and ourselves, rather than trusting others for our well-being?

No one questions that walking barefoot is good for our health. All the nerve centers are represented in our feet and are stimulated by walking. Putting your body in contact with the earth through these nerve endings can be beneficial to your health as well as your morale. Feet are not assisted by shoes to make the natural effort their primary function.

12. The Art of Doing Nothing

In the movie *Eat Pray Love* they speak of the art of doing nothing. It made me realize that doing nothing really is something of an art form, especially in this day and age.

It seems we are always on the go, with a million things to do. But do you ever find that if a slot opens up in your day, maybe your dental hygienist had a family emergency, maybe your client called in sick at the last minute, and suddenly you've got an hour of FREE time, you are confused? What do you do with that hour?

I will speak for myself. Normally, my first thought is: *Yay, a free hour! There is SO much I can do, so much I can catch up on!* I will mentally scan my to-do list, then physically scan my smart phone's ongoing to-do list and try to figure out how much I can squeeze into this free hour. Suddenly the free hour has turned into just another part of the 'go-go-go' day.

Why Can't We Stop?

Why don't I just stop? Maybe go outside for some fresh air? Maybe- dare I say it – nap (the ultimate mommy faux pas)?

I remember one morning I was speaking with my sister on the phone, sprawled out on my bed. Even though I had a million things to do, I chose to just lay there and be on the phone. Unfortunately, a part of me was embarrassed to admit it. Why? What happened in our lives that someone decided that the more we do and we take on and the thinner we spread ourselves, the more we should be praised? It is what I call the 'martyr syndrome.' Should it not be the opposite? Should we not be admiring those living a full, yet relaxed and stress-free existence? Should that not be our goal, instead of working more to acquire more stuff that we never have time to play with anyway?

I remember going to Italy and thinking: *yep, they have it all figured out: everything shuts down on Sundays, they take midday siestas and walks on cobblestone paths and lunches at the bistro. Totally 'chillaxed'.*

I know we are busy, I know we have jobs (some of us more than one), kids' activities, school, cooking, cleaning, events, and, and, and. But maybe, just maybe, occasionally we can stop for five or six minutes a day, and do nothing, absolutely nothing, and more importantly, not feel guilty about it. Maybe we do not need to jam-pack never-ending activities into one week? And if you are a scheduling to the minute person, then schedule in 'nothing time'. You can do it. And when nothing time comes around, as my friend Dianne says: "power down." Shut off your phone, or at least put it on silent, walk away from it and just do nothing. But really do nothing: no television; no video games; no stimulation. Just you, your breathing and your thoughts: complete Bliss Buzz.

Try it out. You might find, as I do, that the art of doing nothing makes you more effective at doing everything else. Imagine that.

13. Her Name Was Robert?

My children and I were at a show in Toronto. There was an endless line-up of what seemed like thousands of people.

Everyone who knows me can tell you I make it a point to address people I have just met by their first name. Even if it is someone checking me out at the grocery store, I like to read their nametag or ask their name, and when thanking them address them by their name. It helps me to feel connected. I like connections. All of a sudden, aisle number nine becomes Ashley.

When I worked in the travel and tourism industry, for most of my positions I had a nametag (hotels, tour operators, etc.) I knew I had them on, but every time someone addressed me by my name, without fail, I was taken aback and I felt just that much happier.

"How did you know my name?"

"It's on your name tag!"

Hilarious!

It always made me happy because in that instant, I was no longer just another guest service agent or person in a cubicle, I was Ioana.

I know that we, as humans, yearn to be unique. Why? In psychology there is something called an Optimal Distinctiveness Theory. The optimal distinctiveness theory states that individuals need to fulfill two competing needs: the need to belong or assimilate, and the need to feel distinct and unique. As reviewed by Lynn and Snyder (2002), individuals experience anxiety when they are informed their characteristics are not unique, but overlap with the traits and attributes of someone else. More recent studies have also corroborated this need to feel unique. Simsek and Yalincetin (2010) developed a measure that can be administered to assess whether or not this need to feel unique is fulfilled. The scale comprises five items such as "I feel that some of my characteristics are completely unique to me" and "As people get to know me more, they begin to recognize some of my special features." More importantly, Simsek and Yalincetin (2010) showed this feeling of uniqueness was positively associated with measures of wellbeing. Specifically, when individuals felt unique, they were more likely to experience hope in their lives, as well as report resilience. Finally, this feeling of uniqueness was inversely related to depression and anxiety.[xxx]

I am always reminded of the theme song of Cheers, *Sometimes you wanna go where everybody knows your name.* A classic, and with good reason: it's absolutely true!

Conversely, walking into a giant establishment and feeling like just another number can be impersonal and cold. As an example, I believe this to be one of the reasons people may choose a studio over a gym.

Ok, now back to the show in Toronto. We walked in and I said to one of the young ladies greeting us and providing us with some items we needed for the show: "Hey Robert, you look a lot like a girl!" She looked at me and smiled. Her name tag read "Robert."

She said, "Do you know that you are the first person to notice that today? I have been wearing this name tag all day!"

That shocked me and made me a little sad. How is that possible? Hundreds, maybe thousands of people must have walked in those doors. Are people in such a hurry nowadays? Or am I not the norm wanting to address people by their first name?

I used to make it a point to ask the name of each and every person who walks into my studio or any of the classes I teach around the country. Will I remember them all? Probably not. But I try, and guess what? When I remember Janice's name the next week, she is not only impressed, but connected. Because she is magically no longer just another participant, she is Janice. Janice whose sister is Karen; Janice who is beautiful but thinks her thighs are hideous; Janice who does not like to look at herself in the mirror. I would have never thought any of that to look at Janice. More importantly, I would have never known that if I did not reach out to Janice. You just never know. And how can you until you make a connection?

So the next time your items are being scanned through the checkout, maybe read that person's nametag and address them, maybe even ask them how their day has been, maybe even compliment them on something they are wearing. Watch their demeanor completely transform because suddenly, you have acknowledged that Donna is a human being not a robot. It seems logical, but if it is then why don't more people do it? They may find they will get a two way Bliss Buzz from something so simple.

As for the Toronto show, the actual owner of the nametag, Robert, was also walking around with the wrong nametag: hers! I wonder if he had more luck.

14. Don't Be Ashamed – Just Mindful!

This is a short chapter, but I had to include it as I feel it is something many of us experience, to a certain extent, at some point in our lives.

I was having a typical conversation with some women on an online health forum one day. The topic was coffee. One woman mentioned the benefits of coffee but pointed out that all the other "bad stuff" (sugar, cream) should not be added. In response to this, another woman said she was ashamed to admit that she herself adds all that bad stuff.

Stop right there!

Andrew Facca, creator of the *Voyage to Betterment, The Body Mind Spirit Challenge* and *the Facca Way* once said in a lecture that I attended, that even if you are consuming something you know is bad for you, or is not necessarily the healthiest of food choices, you should not be mad at it. Instead, you should eat it with love and gratitude. After all there are so many people around the world who cannot even afford the luxury of choice.

That really resonated with me. So many times, we feel angry or guilty about our decisions. When we do this, it only leads to a downward spiral of bad decisions, coupled with the unhealthy side effects of emotional torment.

In my humble opinion, one of the fundamentals of our health journey is mindfulness. What can harm us more than our poor choices is their denial.

I am a holistic nutritionist. Do you think I eat perfectly healthy 100% of the time? Nope. I will on occasion eat French fries *gasp*. But I am aware of the health detriments, it is not a staple in my diet, and I am at peace with that. I am aware of what goes into my body but try (I too am a work in progress) not to give myself grief over my decisions. At our home we (my three kids, husband, and myself), try to follow the 80/20 rule. We eat like holistic rock stars 80% of the time while giving ourselves a 20% margin to eat the not so awesome stuff.

Nobody is perfect, or at least nobody I have ever met. To spend our lives judging others and ourselves seems a bit hypocritically bizarre and an awful waste of time and energy.

Just be aware, be mindful, be open, and allow yourself that Bliss Buzz at every meal...and bon appétit!

15. Vibrations Vibrations Vibrations

Do you ever notice that when you are around certain people you cannot help but be happy, feel a sense of comfort, even peace? These people likely emit high vibrations.

What happens when you are in a traffic jam and someone starts to beep, triggering a chain reaction? Other people begin to swear, act offensively and aggressively. Do you feel your blood pressure rise? These are low vibrations.

I am no expert, but I do know with 100% certainty that surrounding yourself with positive and high vibrations makes you vibrate at a higher level.

I am blessed in what I do to frequently be surrounded by positivity. People attending my classes arrive with positive intentions, so they rock my chakras top to bottom. I believe positivity is contagious and nothing is more delicious than positive on positive on positive.

I am aware, however, that some people have the misfortune of being in lower vibration situations. A job they do not like, an abusive relationship, etc. What can they do? In my humble opinion these people should surround themselves as much as possible with positive, inspirational people and situations. Vibrations do not stop at people. Food also has vibrations, as does the earth. This is one of the reasons we feel exhilarated in nature.

The Law of Vibration

The Law of Vibration might not be as well-known as the Law of Attraction. However, the Law of Vibration serves as the foundation for the Law of Attraction.

To understand this, it is important to know that everything is energy. Science, through Quantum Physics, is showing us that everything in our universe is energy.

When we go down on a sub-atomic level we do not find matter, but pure energy. Some called this the unified field or the matrix. Others talk about pure potentiality: all being energy.

Everything Vibrates

This Universal Law states that everything in the universe moves and vibrates; everything is vibrating at one speed or another. Nothing rests. Everything you see around you is vibrating at one frequency or another, and so are you. However, your frequency is different from other things in the universe. Hence, it seems like you are separated from what you see around you: people, animals, plants, trees, and so on. BUT you are not separated; you are in fact living in an ocean of energy. We all are. We are all connected at the lowest level, a level, professor John Hagelin calls, the unified field.

Setting Your Vibrational Tone

Back in 1986 Esther and her husband Jerry Hicks came into contact with non-physical entities called Abraham. Abraham is a group of evolved teachers from "the other side." These non-physical entities speak through Esther. The Law of Vibration is the law that serves as the foundation for the Law of Attraction.

Everything has its own vibrational frequency: the table, the car, the picture frame, the rock, even our thoughts and feelings. It is all governed by The Law of Vibration.

A table may look solid and still, but within the table are millions of millions of subatomic particles running around and popping with energy. The table is pure energy and movement. Everything in this universe has its own vibrational frequency. It is The Law of Vibration in action. However, we can't see it so it appears separate and solid to us. It is actually an illusion.

The Law of Vibration is real. Even if you can't see it, it does not mean that it is not true.

Believing Is Seeing

Before the invention of the microscope, people would have labelled you totally crazy if you told them that small "creatures crawled around" on the skin of all human beings.

Why?

Simply because people could not see them.

Today, we all know that our skin is covered with bacteria. It appears that the skin, the largest organ in our body, is a kind of zoo.

According to a study in 2007 performed by the Department of Medicine at NYU School of Medicine, researchers found evidence for 182 species of bacteria in skin samples.

If you had told this to people before the invention of the microscope, they would have locked you up and thrown away the key. Today we don't even bother thinking about all these bacteria, these "creatures" living off our skin.

Before the invention of the Electron microscope in 1931, which made it possible to view objects as small as the diameter of an atom, no-one believed there could exist something so small.

Humans live by the old saying "seeing is believing" but why do we not learn from history and realize that something might be true even though we do not see it? We do not have to see something to believe it.

It should be the other way around; believing will make you see. Most people only choose to look at what they know now and what they can see. They only rely on their five senses. They are not willing to keep an open mind. They are not willing to accept that everything vibrates and that

The Law of Vibration is real; that we are vibrating sending-towers transmitting our thoughts and feelings into the universe all the time.

Frame of Knowledge

Most people are only looking inside our frame of knowledge. In other words, they only relate to what they can see, verify, and test. They rely only on their 5 senses to tell them what their reality is. They are only using their sensory level to define their frame of knowledge in the time we are living.

This frame however, seems to change when science can tell us that something is true.

Before It Was a "Fact" That the Earth Was Flat

But as we know now it wasn't; it is round.

Then the Earth was the center of the universe, but it wasn't; then The Milky-Way was the only galaxy, but it wasn't. It was only one of billions of galaxies.

Our frame of knowledge is constantly changing since science is showing us "new" truths. Our frame of knowledge has been changing as long as we have lived on this planet.

It is about time we realize that something can be a reality even though we can't use our 5 senses to verify it.

Keep an Open Mind

Let us use the dog-whistle as an example to illustrate a point about what we perceive as true or not. Today, we all know that dogs can detect sounds that are undetectable to the human ear.

When someone blows a dog-whistle we know that the sounds from that dog-whistle will be detected by the dog, even though we can't hear it. Our 5 senses are not able to detect the sound, but still we accept this as fact, as true, as our reality.

Why?

Because science has shown us that dogs can detect sounds we can't. Before science could prove it, we did not believe it to be true.

We need to open up to the idea that there are things in our lives going on which might be true even though we can't use our 5 senses to verify it, like the Law of Vibration.

We need to keep an open mind and we should be better at thinking out of the box. We ought to realize that what we think is impossible today might be obvious and a known fact in 10-15 years time. The Law of Vibration might be a subject in school for children to learn about just like the Law of Gravity.

Today no-one questions the use of the cell phone making it possible to talk to other people on the other side of the planet without a wire to be seen; it is all wireless.

You can't see how it works, but you believe in it since science told you it works. Then you tried it out for yourselves.

We can reach out to millions of people through the Internet and no-one questions that either because it is technology of our time. On the other hand, if someone told you 40 years ago that you would be able to surf something called the Internet and you could reach millions of people using this Internet with extremely low cost, you would not believe it.

Why?

Because it would not be part of your frame of knowledge at that time in history.

If someone told you 100 years ago that you could carry with you a tiny gadget with the capacity to store thousands of songs, take pictures, and enable you to talk to someone on the other side of the planet wireless, you would think they were totally crazy. Today, iPhone and similar phones with all these features are as common as milk and bread to many people all over the globe.

Radio Waves

Inventors throughout history have had a hard time being accepted and believed by their fellow man when they invented something new.

Why?

Because the frame of knowledge at that time did not have the ability to grasp it. The inventors and pioneers throughout history have made new ground. However, many people are afraid of changing what they already know. Hence, these inventors and pioneers, being ahead of their time, have been struggling to be heard.

Guglielmo Marconi was an Italian inventor and he was able to show to the world the feasibility of radio communication. However, he had a hard time being believed that signals could be sent wireless. His colleagues and other scientists said he was ready for the "looney-house."

He sent and received his first radio signal in Italy in 1895. By 1899 he flashed the first wireless signal across the English Channel.

On June 2nd 1896, Marconi applied for a British wireless telegraphy patent. Shortly thereafter, he applied for and obtained a patent in the United States. He electrified the world when he succeeded in sending a wireless signal from

Newfoundland to Ireland. Believing that radio waves, like light rays, on which signals had already been sent, shot out into space when they reached the horizon, some scientists did not believe his claim to have sent a signal across the Atlantic.

Today we know better.

However, Marconi was NOT the first one to discover radio waves even though most people think so. Most of us think of Guglielmo Marconi as the father of radio, and we know little of Nikola Tesla's work in radio.

Marconi claimed all the first patents for radio, something originally developed by Tesla. Nikola Tesla tried to prove that he was the creator of radio but it wasn't until 1943 that Marconi's patents were deemed invalid. However, people still have no idea about Tesla's work with radio.

Will We Change What We Believe In?

Maybe 15 years from now the Law of Vibration will be a well-known fact for every single person on this planet, just as much a fact as our planet being round and part of the Milky Way. Maybe it will be part of the teaching in every school and the kids will learn how to send out positive thoughts and vibrations as part of their behavior. They will learn to understand The Law of Vibration, The Law of Attraction and other universal Laws governing our lives.

We need to believe that anything is possible. We just need to believe it. Believing is seeing.

So believe in The Law of Vibration: that everything is vibrating. Absolutely everything. We are actually living in a sea of energy, or to quote Bob Proctor from *The Secret*:

"We live in an ocean of motion."

Our thoughts are on a certain vibrational frequency and hence are part of the vibrating universe. The Law of Attraction, which is based on The Law of Vibration, states that we attract what we are sending out. Hence, positive energies attract positive energies and negative energies attract negative energies.

Our thoughts are cosmic waves of energy that penetrate all time and space. Thought is the most potent vibration; this means you can attract to you what you want and wish for.

Learn about the Power of Thought and how thoughts make ripples in the sea of energy we call the universe, consciousness, the formula for success, universal Laws, and more by getting the free *Make a Ripple Make a Difference* e-book

In 1910 Wallace D. Wattles wrote *The Science of Getting Rich*.

He speaks of a thinking "stuff" from which all things are made:

"Everything you see on Earth is made from one original substance, out of which all things proceed."

There is a thinking stuff from which all things are made, and which, in its original state, permeates, penetrates, and fills the interspaces of the universe.

A thought, in this substance, produces the thing that is imaged by thought.

Man can form things in his thought, and, by impressing his thought upon formless substance, can cause the thing he thinks about to be created.

The Law of Attraction and the Law of Vibration Go Hand in Hand

When you know that your thoughts and emotions are vibrating (Law of Vibration) and you know that like attracts like (Law of Attraction), you will appreciate that you can now start to alter your life just by altering your thoughts and emotions.

Unfortunately, many of us are "programmed" from childhood to have thoughts and emotions about worry, fear, scarcity, and so on.

If you change these patterns of thoughts and feelings, you will be able to attract into your life what you truly want.

Mike Dooley is an author with the bestselling book The Art of Living Your Dream. He is also the founder of Notes from the Universe which are short emails with often humorous reminders of life's magic and your divinity. In one of his Notes he talks about how we should think of our dreams as though they have already happened. This of course is one of the key elements of the Law of Attraction in order to send out the right vibrations (The Law of Vibration).

Just once a day, imagine the life you dream of. Believe that it can be yours in this world of magic and miracles. Choose to live as if you know of its inevitable manifestation. Don't compromise. Don't worry. Don't look for results. And as surely as spirit crafts one moment after another, so too will it fuse together the life you now lead with the life of your dreams, as if they were two pieces of a jigsaw puzzle, destined to become one.

So, why have many people failed at getting what they wish for? Why doesn't the Law of Attraction work?

It does work as long as you send out the right vibrations. The Law of Vibration never fails. Everything vibrates. Experts in the Law of Attraction say that you must do more than just make a wish.

Your emotions and feelings must also be aligned with what you wish for. It is not enough to merely ask for it if you do not truly have emotions and feelings that are in harmony with that wish. You need to fall in love with what you want in order to be in the correct vibrational state.

If you ask for more money through prayer, meditation, or just by wanting it, it will not help you if your emotions and feelings are programmed to think that money does not grow on trees, or that you do not deserve to be rich, or that you cannot handle being rich, etc.

If you grew up in a family where your father or mother (or both) always said, "Do you think I am made out of money? We can't afford that"; then most likely, you are programmed to believe this to be true.

Your subconscious mind has a different belief system than what you are wishing for. Hence your inner feelings and emotions are not aligned with your wish. These beliefs are thousands of times stronger than desires and wishes. So if you desire something like a new house or getting a new job, it will not happen if your beliefs are "I can't'." The beliefs win every time.

We all have built a blueprint in our mind (subconscious) of what we regard as true and what we believe in. This blueprint has been sculpted for years through your childhood by your father and mother, by your brothers and sisters, by your friends, by what you read in the newspapers, by what you see on TV, by what you learn in school, and so on.

If suddenly new information is presented to this blueprint, it will not automatically be added. You can ask for more money every day for several years and nothing will ever manifest because, as the Law of Attraction preaches, your subconscious is not aligned with that desire. This is the reason why so many people who attempt to change their lives by using the Law of Attraction fail.

In order to change your belief system you can start applying affirmations.

Reprogram your subconscious mind with a new belief system. Believe that anything is possible. Believe that you are rich, that you deserve to be rich, that you are happy, that you are healthy, and so on. Make a list of positive affirmations and read them to yourself every day. Say to yourself those things you want to be or believe in.

Subliminal Messages

Many people also use subliminal messages together with quiet music that enhance connection between the right and the left hemisphere of the brain. Embedded in the music are affirmations about good health, or financial wealth, or happiness, and so on. Subliminal messages have been successful for many years helping people change their lives.[xxxi]

A positive person, some deliciously high vibrating healthy foods, a positive environment, nature - yes gorgeous, high energy nature, I believe these can help offset the negative. Seems pretty straightforward right? It can't possibly be that simple can it? It is. Sometimes it is simply that simple. And sometimes simplicity is blissful.

Enjoy your Bliss Buzz vibrations.

16. The Evolution of the Resolution

I worked at a gym for years, and for years, I found it fascinating that at the beginning of the year there was such a massive influx of memberships and members anxious to get on the machines and attend classes, only to dissipate a few short months later. I am not sure what the statistics are but the dropout rate of attendance between January and April in gyms is fascinating and shocking all at once.

What's the story? I'm not a psychologist but my theory is that anytime you put a timeline on your lifestyle or health (i.e. on January 1st I will begin and by June 1st will have a bikini body) the mind immediately goes into adrenaline, anxiety, and pressure mode. The problem with that is, as soon as the adrenaline and all the extras wear off, so does the temporary lifestyle resolution.

I used to be in that boat: binge, binge, binge because on Monday or January 1st I will be 'good.' The problem with that is that the pressure that we place on ourselves is so high that when we falter we just as easily throw in the towel.

This is nothing you have not heard before.

What I do believe, because of my personal experience and observations over the years, is that we simply need to be convinced of why we are choosing a healthier lifestyle. Weight loss? Wrong. Appearance? Wrong. No ego motivators are ever, in my humble opinion, what will lead to our ultimate happiness. At the end of the day, the desire to have that piece of chocolate or satisfy the taste will easily overrule the superficial. Instant gratification is a powerful entity.

I realized that as soon as I gave myself a deadline (ex. *I need to lose 10lbs by November 1*), I got hungry. Conversely, as soon as I say to myself: *You can eat anything you want on the 1st of January*, I am suddenly not as hungry anymore. Enough said.

Here's a whimsical thought: let us decide to just always be as healthy as we can be because it feels awesome; because we can move better; because we can dance better; because we feel better; because we can run around better; because we can play more energetically with our kids; because we can be more productive at work; because we can sleep better. Yes as females we might, and most likely will, always want to be pretty, and that's ok, but let that not be the motivator or a destructive obsession.

Be motivated by how you feel and resolve to do that 24/7, January to December. Be a fulltime-balanced lover of life, not a part time health-radical.

This is the evolution of the resolution, *and I'm feelin' good* (sing it to the tune of Michael Bublé).

17. Eat, Stay, Love

I finally watched the movie *Eat, Pray, Love* and I was left with a lingering question mark. I could not quite put my finger on it. Then, not long after, in having a conversation with a friend it dawned on me, one important truth is that while escape may be the solution, it is not always an option for everyone. At the end of the movie, Julia Roberts ends up living in an exotic part of the world with the man of her dreams and does not return to her mundane life. It is phenomenal she was able to do that, and I do know many people who have picked up and just left. However, the truth of the matter is that so many people cannot do that for one reason or another. Maybe they are the caregiver to a parent, maybe they have a huge family to support and their job pays the bills.

So many people cannot simply pick up and escape their lives. What can they do if they feel the need to? The solution is to figure out how to do all the fabulous things in the movie here and now. We all eat, so we should really enjoy and appreciate our foods. Most of us love at least one person in our lives, so let's love them fully and with our souls, and maybe tell them we love them over and over again. We can all afford five minutes a day to stop, just as I mentioned in the chapter on the art of doing nothing. We can pick up the phone and talk to a friend who we usually text. We can schedule a tea date with a friend we have not seen in a year. Take a bath. Eat vibrant happy food, food that is so colorful we just want to stare at it and take a picture of it. And we will do that because it makes us feel good. And maybe even we can sit down and remove all stimulation while we are eating. People can still show up to their 9 to 5 jobs that they dislike, but they will show up happier. And when they return home they can get back to the things that bring them vitality: a run; a jog; a brisk walk; a bike ride; journaling; knitting; dancing; painting. Have you ever tried finger painting? Try it. Why? Why not? If you have children or pets, engage in activities with them. Meditate with them. Dance with them. Sing with them, or sing to them. Then, for no reason at all: LOL (laugh out loud). Not via text or Facebook but in real time, face-to-face. Really laugh out loud!

You can do all this here and now. Not yesterday, not tomorrow, or on the other side, or at that resort across the globe. Right now. Eat, Love, Stay.

18. Meditate Your Way to Your Bliss Buzz

I always tell my clients that meditation can be or mean so many things to different people. To some people meditation is sitting still in lotus position chanting. For others, it may be laying on their backs, feeling the rise and fall of their belly as they listen to inspiring music or guided visualization. To you, it may be stillness or movement. Meditation simply brings you to a state of peace and tranquility, and if you are lucky, it can restructure and gradually eliminate your negative thoughts.

How Meditation Changes Your Brain: A Neuroscientist Explains by Dr. Sarah McKay

Do you struggle, like me, with monkey mind? Is your brain also a little unsettled, restless, capricious, whimsical, fanciful, inconstant, confused, indecisive, or uncontrollable? That's the definition of "monkey mind" I've been given!

If you need more motivation to take up this transformative practice, neuroscience research has shown that meditation and mindfulness training can cause neuroplastic changes to the gray matter of your brain.

A group of Harvard neuroscientists interested in mindfulness meditation have reported that brain structures change after only eight weeks of meditation practice.

Sara Lazar, Ph.D., the study's senior author, said in a press release, "Although the practice of meditation is associated with a sense of peacefulness and physical relaxation, practitioners have long claimed that meditation also provides cognitive and psychological benefits that persist throughout the day."

To test their idea, the neuroscientists enrolled 16 people in an eight-week mindfulness based stress reduction course. The course promised to improve participants' mindfulness and well-being, and reduce their levels of stress.

Everyone received audio recordings containing 45 minute guided mindfulness exercises (body scan, yoga, and sitting meditation) that they were instructed to practice daily at home. And to facilitate the integration of mindfulness into daily life, they were also taught to practice mindfulness informally in everyday activities such as eating, walking, washing the dishes, taking a shower, and so on. On average, the meditation group participants spent an average of 27 minutes a day practicing some form of mindfulness.

Magnetic resonance images (MRI scans) of everyone's brains were taken before and after they completed the meditation training, and a control group of people who didn't do any mindfulness training also had their brains scanned.

After completing the mindfulness course, all participants reported significant improvement in measures of mindfulness, such as "acting with awareness" and "non-judging."

What was startling was that the MRI scans showed that mindfulness groups increased gray matter concentration within the left hippocampus, the posterior cingulate cortex, the temporo-parietal junction, and the cerebellum. Brain regions involved in learning and memory, emotion regulation, sense of self, and perspective taking!

Britta Hölzel, the lead author on the paper says,

"It is fascinating to see the brain's plasticity and that, by practicing meditation, we can play an active role in changing the brain and can increase our well-being and quality of life."

Sarah Lazar also noted,

"This study demonstrates that changes in brain structure may underlie some of these reported improvements and that people are not just feeling better because they are spending time relaxing."[xxxii]

This Is Your Brain on Meditation

The Science Explaining Why You Should Meditate Every Day by Rebecca Gladding, M.D. in *Use Your Mind to Change Your Brain:*

I realized today that in all my posts regarding the brain and how to sculpt it with mindfulness, I've never actually explained how and why meditation works. Specifically, the science behind how your brain changes the longer you meditate. I think this is important for many reasons, but one of the most salient is that this information serves as a great motivator to keep up a daily practice (or start one).

I'm sure you've heard people extol the virtues of meditation. You may be skeptical of the claims that it helps with all aspects of life. But, the truth is, it does. Sitting every day, for at least 15-30 minutes, makes a huge difference in how you approach life, how personally you take things, and how you interact with others. It enhances compassion, allows you to see things more clearly (including yourself), and creates a sense of calm and centeredness that is indescribable. There really is no substitute.

For those of you who are curious as to how meditation changes the brain, this is for you. Although this may be slightly technical, bear with me because it's really interesting. The brain, and how we are able to mold it, is fascinating and nothing short of amazing. Here are the brain areas you need to know:

- *Lateral prefrontal cortex: the part of the brain that allows you to look at things from a more rational, logical, and balanced perspective. In the book, we call it the* **Assessment Center.** *It is involved in modulating* *emotional responses (originating from the fear center or other parts of the brain), overriding automatic behaviors/habits and decreasing the brain's tendency to take things personally (by modulating the Me Center of the brain, see below).*

- *Medial prefrontal cortex: the part of the brain that constantly references back to you, your perspective, and experiences. Many people call this the **"Me Center"** of the brain because it processes information related to you, including when you are daydreaming, thinking about the future, reflecting on yourself, engaging in social interactions, inferring other people's state of mind or feeling empathy for others. We call it the Self-Referencing Center.*

What's interesting about the Medial PreFrontal Cortex (mPFC) is that it actually has two sections:

- *Ventromedial medial prefrontal cortex (vmPFC) – involved in processing information related to you and people that you view as similar to you. This is the part of the brain that can cause you to end up taking things too personally, which is why we referred to it as the unhelpful aspect of the Self-Referencing Center in the book. (In reality, this brain area has many important and helpful functions – since we were focusing on overcoming anxiety, depression and habits you want to change, we referred to it as unhelpful because it often causes increases in rumination/worry and exacerbates anxious or depressive thoughts/states/feelings.)*

- *Dorsomedial Prefrontal Cortex (dmPFC) – involved in processing information related to people who you perceive as being dissimilar from you. This very important part of the brain is involved in feeling empathy (especially for people who we perceive of as not being like us) and maintaining social connections.*

- *Insula: the part of the brain that monitors **bodily sensations** and is involved in experiencing "gut-level" feelings. Along with other brain areas, it helps "guide" how strongly you will respond to what you sense in your body (i.e., is this sensation something dangerous or benign?). It is also heavily involved in experiencing/feeling empathy.*

- *Amygdala: the alarm system of the brain, what most refer to as the **"Fear Center."** It's a part of the brain that is responsible for many of our initial emotional responses and reactions, including the "fight-or-flight" response. (Along with the Insula, this is what we referred to as the Uh Oh Center.)*

The Brain without Meditation – Stuck on Me

If you were to look at people's brains before they began a meditation practice, you would likely see strong neural connections within the Me Center, and between the Me Center and the bodily sensation/fear centers of the brain. This means that whenever you feel anxious, scared, or have a sensation in your body (e.g., a tingling, pain, itching, whatever), you are far more likely to assume that there is a problem (related to you or your safety). This is precisely because the Me Center is processing the bulk of the information. What's more, this over-reliance on the Me Center explains how it is that we often get stuck in repeating loops of thought about our life, mistakes we made, how people feel about us, our bodies (e.g., "I've had this pain before, does this mean something serious is going on?"), and so on.

Why is the Me Center allowed to process information this way, essentially unabated? The reason this happens, in part, is because the Assessment Center's connection to the Me Center is relatively weak. If the Assessment Center was working at a higher capacity, it would modulate the excessive activity of the vmPFC (the part that takes things personally) and enhance the activity of the dmPFC (the part involved in understanding other's thoughts and feelings). This would lead us to take in all the relevant information, discard erroneous data (that the Me Center might want to focus on exclusively) and view whatever is happening from a more balanced perspective – essentially decreasing the overthinking, ruminating, and worrying that the Me Center is famous for promulgating. One helpful way to think of the Assessment Center is as a sort of "brake" for the unhelpful parts of the Me Center.

The Brain on Meditation – I Can See Clearly Now

In contrast, if you meditate on a regular basis, several positive things happen. First, the strong, tightly held connection between the Me Center (specifically the unhelpful vmPFC) and the bodily sensation/fear centers begins to break down. As this connection withers, you will no longer assume that a bodily sensation or momentary feeling of fear means something is wrong with you or that you are the problem! This explains, in part, why anxiety decreases the more you meditate – it's because the neural paths that link those upsetting sensations to the Me Center are decreasing. Said another way, your ability to ignore sensations of anxiety is enhanced as you begin to break that connection between the unhelpful parts of the Me Center and the bodily sensation/fear centers. As a result, you are more readily able to see those sensations for what they are and not respond as strongly to them (thanks to your strengthened Assessment Center).

Second, a heftier, healthier connection forms between the Assessment Center and bodily sensation/fear centers. This means that when you experience a bodily sensation or something potentially dangerous or upsetting, you are able to look at it from a more rational perspective (rather than automatically reacting and assuming it has something to do with you). For example, when you experience pain, rather than becoming anxious and assuming it means something is wrong with you, you can watch the pain rise and fall without becoming ensnared in a story about what it might mean.

Finally, an added bonus of meditating is that the connection between the helpful aspects of the Me Center (i.e., dorsomedial prefrontal cortex) – the part involved in processing information related to people we perceive as being not like us – and the bodily sensation center – involved in empathy – becomes stronger. This healthy connection enhances your capacity to understand where another person is coming from, especially those who you cannot intuitively understand because you think or perceive things differently from them (i.e., dissimilar others). This increased connection explains why meditation enhances empathy – it helps us use the part of the brain that infers other people's states of mind, their motivations, desires, dreams, and so on, while simultaneously activating the part of the brain involved in the actual experience of empathy (insula). The end result is that we are more able to put ourselves in another person's shoes (especially those not like us), thereby increasing our ability to feel empathy and compassion for everyone.

Daily Practice Is Important Essentially, the science "proves" what we know to be true from the actual experience of meditating. What the data demonstrate is that meditation facilitates strengthening the Assessment Center, weakening the unhelpful aspects of the Me Center (that can cause you to take things personally), strengthening the helpful parts of the Me Center (involved with empathy and understanding others), and changing the connections to/from the bodily sensation/fear centers such that you experience sensations in a less reactive, more balanced, and holistic way. In a very real way, you literally are changing your brain for the better when you meditate.

In the end, this means that you are able to see yourself and everyone around you from a clearer perspective, while simultaneously being more present, compassionate, and empathetic with people no matter the situation. With time and practice, people do truly become calmer, have a greater capacity for empathy, and find they tend to respond in a more balanced way to things, people, or events in their lives.

However, to maintain your gains, you have to keep meditating. Why? Because the brain can very easily revert back to its old ways if you are not vigilant (I'm referencing the idea of neuroplasticity here). This means you have to keep meditating to ensure that the new neural pathways you worked so hard to form stay strong.

To me, this amazing brain science and the very real rewards gained from meditation combine to form a compelling argument for developing and/or maintaining a daily practice. It definitely motivates me on those days I don't "feel" like sitting. So, try to remind yourself that meditating every day, even if it's only 15 minutes, will keep those newly formed connections strong and those unhelpful ones of the past at bay.

Addendum: For those wanting to start a meditation practice or who might be experiencing emotional issues, memories, etc. when meditating, please seek out an experienced meditation teacher. I have received some comments from people stating they do not believe meditation works (which is likely true for some people) or that it could be harmful if done incorrectly. Obviously, meditation has been very positive for me, but I have always worked with a meditation teacher or mentor and I would suggest you do the same, as a teacher can help you figure out what is right for you and guide you through any difficulties you may be having.[xxxiii]

Brain scans show meditation changes minds and increases attention.

For hundreds of years, Tibetan monks and other religious people have used meditation to calm the mind and improve concentration. This week, a new study shows exactly how one common type of meditation affects the brain.

Using a scanner that reveals which parts of the brain are active at any given moment, the researchers found that meditation increased activity in the brain regions used for paying attention and making decisions.

"Most people, if they heard a baby screaming, would have some emotional response," Davidson says, but not the highly experienced meditators. "They do hear the sound, we can detect that in the auditory cortex, but they don't have the emotional reaction."

The changes were associated with the practice of concentration meditation, says study leader Richard Davidson, professor of psychology and psychiatry at the University of Wisconsin School of Medicine and Public Health and the Waisman Center. Practitioners were instructed to focus attention intently on a stimulus, and when the attention wandered off, to simply bring the attention back to the object, explains Davidson.

"In one sense, concentration mediation is ridiculously simple, but in another, it's extraordinarily difficult," adds Davidson. "If you try it for two minutes, you will see that it's not so easy. Minds have a propensity to wander."

In collaboration with colleagues Julie Brefczynski-Lewis and Antoine Lutz of the UW-Madison W.M. Keck Laboratory for Functional Brain Imaging and Behavior, Davidson compared newly trained meditators to people with up to 54,000 hours of meditation experience. The study is being published this week in the online edition of the Proceedings of the National Academy of Science.

After the novices were taught to meditate, all subjects underwent a magnetic resonance imaging scan of the brain while they were meditating. Among all experienced meditators, the MRI scan found greater activity in brain circuits involved in paying attention.

"We found that regions of the brain that are intimately involved in the control and regulation of attention, such as the prefrontal cortex, were more activated in the long-term practitioners," Davidson says.

A different picture emerged, however, from looking only at the most experienced meditators with at least 40,000 hours of experience. "There was a brief increase in activity as they start meditating, and then it came down to baseline, as if they were able to concentrate in an effortless way," says Davidson.

Effortless concentration is described in classic meditation texts, adds Davidson. "And we think this may be a neural reflection of that. These results illustrate one mechanism by which meditation may act in the brain."

While the subjects meditated inside the MRI, the researchers periodically blasted them with disturbing noises. Among the experienced meditators, the noise had less effect on the brain areas involved in emotion and decision-making than among novice meditators. Among meditators with more than 40,000 hours of lifetime practice, these areas were hardly affected at all.

As Davidson notes, any comparison of average middle-aged Americans to people who have meditated daily for decades must try to associate the differences with meditation, and not lifestyle factors such as isolation or religious faith.

"This was a highly unusual group of people. Two-thirds of the experienced meditators were Tibetan monks, recruited with the help of the Dalai Lama, and they all had an extremely long history of formal practice."

For 15 years, Davidson has had a scientific relationship with the Dalai Lama, spiritual leader of Tibetan Buddhists, to investigate the effects of meditation.

Still, the correlation between more meditation experience and greater brain changes does suggest that the changes were caused by meditation.

"If it were simply lifestyle, we would not expect a very strong correlation with hours of practice," Davidson says.

Other evidence for the neurological benefits of meditation came from a study Davidson reported in May, which showed that three months of meditation training improved the ability to detect a brief visual signal that most people cannot detect. "That was a more definitive kind of evidence, because we were able to track the same people over time," he says.

Psychologists have long considered an adult's capacity to pay attention as relatively fixed, but Davidson says, "Attention can be trained, and in a way that is not fundamentally different than how physical exercise changes the body."

The attention circuits affected by meditation are also involved in attention deficit hyperactivity disorder, which Davidson describes as the most prevalent psychiatric diagnosis among children in our country.

"Our findings suggest that it may, I stress may, be possible to train attention in children with methods derived from these practices," he says.

Davidson says scientific studies of meditation are proving traditional beliefs about the mental benefits of meditation. Yet although meditation is often associated with monks living a life of simplicity, poverty, and prayer, "There is nothing fundamentally mysterious about these practices; they can be understood in hard-nosed western scientific terms."

And, he adds, a growing body of "hard-nosed neuroscience research" is attracting attention to the profound effects of meditation.

"This deserves serious scientific attention," he says. "It also explains why people spend time sitting on the meditation cushion, because of the effects on day-to-day life."

Davidson compares mental practice to physical exercise.

"We all know that if an individual works out on a regular basis, that can change cardiovascular health," he says. "In the same way, these data suggest that certain basic mechanisms of the mind, like attention, can also be trained and improved through systematic practice."

How Does the Brain Work during Meditation?

Using MRI, researchers looked at how meditation influences brain activity.

Meditation types can be divided into two groups: concentrative meditation and nondirective meditation, a Gemini news release reported. Concentrative meditation is when the person focuses on one thought or their breathing to suppress other thoughts, while in nondirective meditation, the individual focuses on their breathing or a sound but allows their mind to wander.

"No one knows how the brain works when you meditate. That is why I'd like to study it," Jian Xu, a physician at St. Olavs Hospital and a researcher at the Department of Circulation and Medical Imaging at NTNU, said in the news release.

The researchers performed MRIs on 14 people who had experience in Acem meditation. The participants performed both nondirective meditation and a "more concentrative meditation task", the news release reported.

The team found that nondirective meditation spurred higher activity in the part of the brain dedicated to "self-related thoughts and feelings."

"I was surprised that the activity of the brain was greatest when the person's thoughts wandered freely on their own, rather than when the brain worked to be more strongly focused," Xu said. "When the subjects stopped doing a specific task and were not really doing anything special, there was an increase in activity in the area of the brain where we process thoughts and feelings. It is described as a kind of resting network. And it was this area that was most active during nondirective meditation."

The findings indicate that nondirective meditation is more effective at clearing the mind and allowing one to process emotions and memories.

"This area of the brain has its highest activity when we rest. It represents a kind of basic operating system, a resting network that takes over when external tasks do not require our attention. It is remarkable that a mental task like nondirective meditation results in even higher activity in this network than regular rest," Svend Davanger, a neuroscientist at the University of Oslo, and co-author of the study, said in the news release.[xxxiv]

19. Your Turn

You now know all about my favorite Bliss Buzzes. It's your turn! What are some of your Bliss Buzzes?

I have left this space for you to journal and write about your Bliss Buzzes. What are they? How do they make you feel?

You can even post pictures of yourself in your Bliss Buzz moments. On days when you might be feeling down, you can refer to this journal. This will hopefully be a reminder of how simple it can be to lift you up, and hopefully by simply recalling these moments, you will experience bliss.

I wish you a lifetime of Bliss Buzzes!

My Bliss Buzz Journal

My Bliss Buzz   **How It Makes Me Feel**

Bliss Journal

Bibliography

[i] Jon Kabat-Zinn. http://www.goodreads.com/author/quotes/8750 (accessed August 3, 2015)

[ii] "Happiness", last modified August 1, 2015. https://en.wikipedia.org/wiki/Happiness (accessed August 3, 2015)

[iii] Wayne Dyer. BrainyQuote.com, Xplore Inc, 2015. http://www.brainyquote.com/quotes/quotes/w/waynedyer173500.html (accessed August 3, 2015)

[iv] Martha Graham. IWon'tDance.com, September 6, 2012. http://iwontdance.com/post/31001730357/nobody-cares-if-you-cant-dance-well-just-get-up (accessed August 3, 2015)

[v] Madeline Knight. "9 Health Benefits of Dance," last modified July 1, 2011. http://www.everydayhealth.com/fitness-pictures/health-benefits-of-dance.aspx#02 (accessed August 3, 2015)

[vi] Edane Padme. "We Are Hip". Kelani Instructor Training Manual, January 2013. Windsor: Kelani International Inc., 2015. 9

[vii] Desy, Phylameana lila, "Water As a Spiritual Element", http://healing.about.com/od/water/a/water_abbond.htm (accessed August 3, 2015)

[viii] Bruce Lee. "A Warrior's Journey", last modified June 25, 2015, https://en.wikiquote.org/wiki/Bruce_Lee (accessed August 3, 2015)

[ix] "Water Meditation", Buddha Dharma Education Association and BuddhaNet, 2008, http://www.buddhanet.net/e-learning/buddhism/meditate/water.htm (accessed August 3, 2015)

[x] Desy, Phylameana lila, "Water As a Spiritual Element", http://healing.about.com/od/water/a/water_abbond.htm (accessed August 3, 2015)

Bibliography

[xi] Margarita Alcantara, M.S.Ac., L.Ac., "Summer Lovin': How Hugs And Kisses Raise Your Vibration And Activate Acupuncture Points", June 19, 2013, http://alcantaraacupuncture.com/summer-lovin-how-hugs-and-kisses-raise-your-vibration-and-activate-acupuncture-points/ (accessed August 8, 2015)

[xii] Stibich, Mark, PHD, "Top Reasons to Smile", last updated March 7, 2015, http://longevity.about.com/od/lifelongbeauty/tp/smiling.htm (accessed August 3, 2015)

[xiii] Horn, Stacy, "Singing Changes your Brain", August6, 2013, http://ideas.time.com/2013/08/16/singing-changes-your-brain/ (accessed August 6, 2015)

[xiv] Shedd, John A., December 9, 2013, http://quoteinvestigator.com/2013/12/09/safe-harbor/ (accessed August 6, 2015)

[xv] Walsch, Neale Donald. BrainyQuote.com, Xplore Inc, 2015. http://www.brainyquote.com/quotes/quotes/n/nealedonal452086.html (accessed August 6, 2015)

[xvi] Walsch, Neale Donald. BrainyQuote.com, Xplore Inc, 2015. http://www.brainyquote.com/quotes/quotes/n/nealedonal452086.html (accessed August 6, 2015)

[xvii] Mills, Patti, http://www.moresingingplease.com/benefits-of-singin, 2015 (accessed August 6, 2015)

[xviii] "Singing is Good for You". Heart Research UK, 2015, http://heartresearch.org.uk/fundraising/singing-good-you (accessed August 6, 2015)

[xix] Shaw, George Bernard. BrainyQuote.com, Xplore Inc, 2015. http://www.brainyquote.com/quotes/quotes/g/georgebern120971.html (accessed August 6, 2015)

[xx] Buettner, Dan. *The Blue Zones*. (Washington: National Geographic, 2008). 253.

Bibliography

[xxi] Hepburn, Audrey. BrainyQuote.com, Xplore Inc, 2015. http://www.brainyquote.com/quotes/quotes/a/audreyhepb413485.html (accessed August 6, 2015)

[xxii] Gandhi, Mahatma. BrainyQuote.com, Xplore Inc, 2015. http://www.brainyquote.com/quotes/quotes/m/mahatmagan1090(accessed August 6, 2015)

[xxiii] Maia Szalavitz, "Helping Others Helps You to Live Longer", August 23, 2013, http://healthland.time.com/2013/08/23/helping-others-helps-you-to-live-longer/ (accessed August 6, 2015)

[xxiv] Allen R. McConnell Ph.D., "Giving really is better than receiving", Dec 25, 2010, https://www.psychologytoday.com/blog/the-social-self/201012/giving-really-is-better-receiving (accessed August 6, 2015)

[xxv] Dietician Cassie, ""Unbrainwash" Yourself", June 4, 2013, http://www.dietitiancassie.com/unbrainwash-yourself/ (accessed August 6, 2015)

[xxvi] "Oliver Twist - Food, Glorious Food Lyrics". LyricZZ.com, http://www.lyriczz.com/lyrics/oliver-twist/84730-food,-glorious-food/ (accessed August 6, 2015)

[xxvii] Maya Dangerfield, "10 Nutrients Scientifically Proven to Make You Feel Awesome", December 31, 2013, http://greatist.com/happiness/nutrients-boost-mood (accessed August 6, 2015)

[xxviii] Jagerhans, October 10, 2009, http://www.urbandictionary.com/define.php?term=barefooting (accessed August 6, 2015)

[xxix] Dr. Mercola, "Grounding: The Potent Antioxidant That Few Know About... And It's Free", June 14, 2013, http://fitness.mercola.com/sites/fitness/archive/2013/06/14/barefoot-running-bad-or-beneficial.aspx (accessed August 6, 2015)

[xxx] Dr Simon Moss, May 1, 2009, "Optimal Distinctiveness Theory",

Bibliography

http://www.psych-it.com.au/Psychlopedia/article.asp?id=239
(accessed August 7, 2015)

xxxi   "The Law of Vibration". One Mind – One Energy. 2015.
http://www.one-mind-one-energy.com/Law-of-vibration.html
(accessed August 7, 2015)

xxxii   Dr. Sarah McKay, "How Meditation Changes Your Brain: A
Neuroscientist Explains ", February 28, 2014,
http://www.mindbodygreen.com/0-12793/how-meditation-changes-your-brain-a-neuroscientist-explains.html (accessed August7, 2015)

xxxiii   Rebecca Gladding M.D., "This Is Your Brain on Meditation", May 22,
2013, http://www.psychologytoday.com/blog/use-your-mind-change-your-brain/201305/is-your-brain-meditation (accessed August 7, 2015)

xxxiv   Rebekah Marcarelli, "How Does The Brain Work During Meditation?
Researchers Find Out Using MRI", May 19, 2014,
http://www.hngn.com/articles/31665/20140519/how-does-the-brain-work-during-meditation-researchers-find-out-using-mri.htm
(accessed August 7, 2015)

Made in the USA
Monee, IL
19 January 2020